D0090479

Make a Difference

Responding to God's Call to Love the World

MELVIN L. CHEATHAM, M.D.

W PUBLISHING GROUP
A Division of Thomas Nelson Publishers
Since 1798

www.wpublishinggroup.com

MAKE A DIFFERENCE

Published by W Publishing Group, a Division of Thomas Nelson, Inc., P.O. Box 141000, Nashville, Tennessee 37214.

The personal stories included in this book are used with permission.

Library of Congress Cataloging-in-Publication Data

Cheatham, Melvin L.
Make a difference : responding to God's call to love the world / by Melvin L. Cheatham.
p. cm.
Includes bibliographical references.
ISBN 0-8499-1824-3
1. Charity. 2. Good works (Theology) I. Title.
BV4639C436 2004
270.8'2'0922–dc22 2004008951

Printed in the United States of America
04 05 06 07 QW 9 8 7 6 5 4 3 2 1

I DEDICATE THIS BOOK to the countless people everywhere who are responding to God's call to bring help and the gospel of Jesus Christ to the world. The names of most of these people are unknown to the majority of other Christians. They do their work of service each day without recognition, with personal sacrifice, and often under conditions of hardship and danger. But God knows their names, and He is leading their work so people in need will receive help, will come to know Jesus Christ as Lord and Savior, and will bring honor and glory to the Lord's name.

Contents

Part 3
The Trust to Believe

Part 4
The Courage to Live

Foreword

YOU WILL NEVER FORGET the remarkable men and women you are about to meet in the pages of this compelling book.

Over a half-century ago, a young man named John F. Kennedy penned a bestseller entitled *Profiles in Courage*. Mel Cheatham's new book might well be called *Profiles in Courage: Part Two*.

From war-torn Kosovo to famine-wracked Ethiopia, Dr. Cheatham introduces us to some of the most courageous and dedicated people imaginable. Most will never make the headlines or appear on television—nor would they want to. But in the midst of the tragedy and hopelessness of our sin-laden world, they are making a difference by touching others with the love of Christ.

This book was not written by a casual observer or aloof journalist. Dr. Cheatham is one of the most gifted and committed Christians I know, and his willingness to use his skills as a top neurological surgeon to serve people in some of the world's toughest places adds authenticity to his important message.

You will find his highly readable narrative

not only exciting and inspiring, but it will also challenge you to reexamine your own life and readjust your priorities in light of God's Word. More than that, it will challenge you to make a difference right where you are, using the gifts God has already given you.

Yes, we can each make a difference, and Mel Cheatham shows us how.

—BILLY GRAHAM

Acknowledgments

I WANT TO BEGIN by offering my thanks to God. There have been so many blessings for which I am deeply thankful to Him. One is my long and healthy life with many opportunities for following in the footsteps of Jesus, bringing help to people in need.

To my wife, Sylvia, I say, "Thank you." Without your love, help, companionship, and encouragement, I can't imagine the past forty-five years. You have been my wife, the mother of our children, and my partner in all things. You have traveled the world with me, from one dangerous place to another—sometimes in military helmet and flak jacket, other times in a surgical gown, and always with love and compassion in your heart.

To Michael, Elizabeth, and Robert, our grown children who have been a blessing from God, and remain our best friends: we thank you for your love. You have always encouraged us and prayed for us even as we have gone to faraway places.

I will be thankful always for the blessing of the wonderful, close friendship I have with Franklin Graham. My admiration and respect for him is without limits, and I stand in awe of how the Lord has used him to bring help to people in a hurting world. Thank you, Franklin, for your friendship, your example, and the inspiration you have given me.

My special thanks to Dr. Billy Graham. I never imagined that I would meet such a man of God, yet I have been blessed with a deep friendship. Thanks also to Ruth Bell Graham for her friendship, example, encouragement, and the blessing of her smile.

There are so many wonderful people at Samaritan's Purse and the Billy Graham Evangelistic Association who have become close friends, I can't name them all. But I do want to thank Donna Lee Toney, one of our closest friends and executive assistant to Franklin Graham. Thank you, Donna, for your advice, help, and friendship.

My thanks to Preston Parrish, a friend I first met seventeen years ago. For all these years, Preston, you have been a close friend and a person I have greatly admired. Your wise counsel and help in editing this book are greatly appreciated.

To Sam Moore, president and CEO of Thomas Nelson, thank you for your friendship and your encouragement. My words of special thanks also go to David Moberg for approaching me to write this book and to Greg Daniel and Ted Squires from the Thomas Nelson and W Publishing Group staff, for assisting me in bringing this book to completion.

I thank my longtime friend Mark Cutshall for the work he did with me in writing my first books for Thomas Nelson a number of years ago, and for the help he gave in the initial book proposal for this one. And my thanks go to Mary Hollingsworth who worked with me on behalf of W Publishing Group in preparing the final manuscript for publication.

Finally, I want to thank all those who have so openly and generously allowed me to use their stories in this book. Through these stories I pray that countless other people in our world will take time to be still and listen so they too may hear God's voice and know He is calling them to make a difference through helping others for His glory.

Introduction

Becoming Humbled Before God

THEY COULD HAVE BEEN my children . . . or yours. Their smiles appeared so infectious, their eyes so bright and alive, but on closer inspection, their facial expressions seemed unreal. These were children in North Korea, a country where millions of people were suffering and dying because of food shortages resulting from damage to crops from two years of terrible flooding followed by a devastating drought. Though I had only seen photographs of these North Korean children, I prayed they might be saved from starvation. As a member of the board of Samaritan's Purse, an international Christian relief organization, I saw a country running out of food, money, and hope. Then an invitation came from the government of North Korea for Franklin Graham, the president of Samaritan's Purse, to assess their flood and drought damage and see if help might be given.

Franklin and I were on our way home from evaluating the needs for medical and dental assistance in Siberia and the opportunities for proclaiming the gospel there, when he received a long-distance telephone call. Turning to me, he said, "Mel, will you make this trip for me?"

Not having any idea where Franklin wanted me to go, I said, "Sure, Franklin." Without further comment or discussion, Franklin said into the phone, "Yes, he'll go."

After he hung up I asked, "Go where, Franklin?"

"North Korea," he answered.

The invitation for a Christian organization to visit North Korea in July 1997 was unusual. The opportunity for impacting the lives of countless hungry, sick, and suffering people in a country technically still at war with America was immense. I was told that once confirmed, the timing of my visit could not be changed. Such an opportunity as this was surely God's plan, and I prayed I would be faithful in doing what I knew He was calling me to do.

My departure for North Korea, by way of Beijing, China, was to be on August 15. The day before I was to go, I received an early morning phone call I didn't want, but couldn't ignore. It was our daughter, Elizabeth, calling from her home in Detroit, Michigan, two thousand miles away—a mother-to-be with disturbing news.

"Mom and Dad, the doctors believe the baby weighs no more than two and-one-half pounds. And even though I'm only seven months along, they believe the only chance for my baby is for them to induce labor as soon as possible. If that is not successful, a Cesarean may even be necessary."

With a father's heart, I listened. Somewhere in the pause that followed, I silently prayed, *Dear Lord, what should I do? My daughter is in trouble, and yet You've led me to go on this trip. I need Your direction.* What was I to do? What would *you* have done? I knew what I wanted to do. I wanted to ignore God's call to travel to North Korea, where a rare, face-to-face meeting with North Korean leaders could bring help that would save the lives of hundreds if not thousands of children and families.

Yet how could I not be at my daughter's side to hold her hand, to join her husband, Paul, and my wife, Sylvia, and to be there for support while the survival of their first child seemed to hang by a prayer? For me as a loving father, not to be there was unthinkable. Not being where my heavenly Father wanted me to be was also unthinkable.

What about you? Have you ever wanted to turn and go your own way? Even when you've heard God calling you with a shout or in what 1 Kings 19:12 says is His "still, small voice"? Have you ever wanted to just run from it all?

With the Lord seemingly silent and with my heart overwhelmed, I needed answers. I needed direction and peace. I needed to know that God was with me and that he would guide me. In my limited human longing, I needed a greater strength that was not my own.

Strangely enough, it was that moment of indecision that mattered. It happened in a thick, confusing fog that caused me to conclude, "There's no way out." With the phone pressed to my ear, I heard my daughter say, "Dad, the only thing you will be able to do for me if you are here at my side is to pray for me and my baby. And you can do that from wherever you are. Go where God has called you to go. Go to North Korea, and the lives of thousands of other people's babies might be saved."

Through Elizabeth's words, I received God's grace. My desire to be with her that day grew as I boarded the plane that carried me and the four hundred or more other passengers high above the Pacific Ocean. My concern grew even more as I telephoned Sylvia shortly into the flight and learned that the induction of Elizabeth's labor was proceeding very slowly.

Again, I prayed. Again, I used the aircraft's satellite telephone to call the hospital in Detroit. Sylvia told me, "Elizabeth's status is the same. Why not call back in about three hours?" I called back in two! But the hospital switchboard operator told me the hour was too late for any incoming calls to be placed to patient rooms. She also refused to give me any information about the condition of my daughter and her baby.

The only thing I could think to do was to impress upon the switchboard operator the fact that I was a doctor. I said, "You don't understand. I am a physician, and I need to have you put my call through to my daughter's room."

Speaking a little more sternly this time, the operator said, "Doctor, perhaps *you* don't understand. No incoming calls are accepted after ten o'clock at night, and it is past that time here in Detroit!"

I was desperate to get an update concerning my daughter and her unborn baby, and I decided I had better let the telephone operator know who I was. So I said, "This is Dr. Cheatham, and I am a clinical professor of neurosurgery. I will really appreciate it if you will put my call through to my daughter's room or at least connect me with someone who can give me some information about her and her baby." Now I felt sure the operator would forward my call immediately, and I even anticipated that she might offer a word or two of apology for having caused some delay in doing so.

But I was wrong! What I heard her say was, "Doctor, it is *you* who doesn't understand. I am the captain of this switchboard, and *I* am the one who decides whether calls go through or not. It is after ten o'clock at night here, and I am *not* placing your call through." Then I heard the loud *click* that told me we were no longer connected.

I returned to my seat and prayed, *Please, God.* I needed whatever faith I had to complete my prayer. When I thought I couldn't go on, I had to think again. For the next eight hours at thirty-five thousand feet, I approached the Lord as a child with the freedom to say, "*Please, God . . .*

As soon as I made my way off the plane in Beijing, China, I rushed to a telephone and called my wife again. "Hello, dear," I heard her say. "You have a new baby granddaughter named Stephanie. She weighs only 2 pounds, 12 ounces, but she is beautiful. Everything is going very well with the baby and with Elizabeth."

I will never forget the happiness, the joy, and the sense of relief I felt in that special moment. Had something happened to my daughter, or had she lost her very premature baby during childbirth, my not having been at her side in her time of need would have haunted me for the rest of my life. My love for Elizabeth knows no bounds, but she knew God was calling me to show His love to people who were suffering and dying in North Korea.

THIS BOOK IS ABOUT *love*. Jesus said in Luke 10:27, "'You shall love the LORD your God with all your heart, with all your soul, with all your strength, and with all your mind,' and 'your neighbor as yourself.'" This book is about ways in which we are to *give* to others as an expression of God's love.

God often calls us to serve Him now—not at a time of our convenience. The place He asks us to go in His service may be right in our own neighborhood, but for some it will be a most unlikely place, perhaps far away. We can know the work God calls us to do will never be beyond our capability to respond. Through that work, the gospel will be presented in action, giving to us the opportunity to lead others to *believe* in Jesus Christ.

God's gift of being able to *live* in this life and throughout eternity is for those who choose to do so through accepting His Son Jesus Christ as Lord and Savior.

If you long to *make a difference* in the lives of others, take time to be still and listen for God's voice. I believe you will hear Him calling you to serve Him and telling you what it is He has planned especially for you. Then you can respond to Him, "Yes, Lord, I'll go; send me." If you do this, you will be led to know His great truth: life becomes full when you begin to give it away.

PART 1

The Call to Love

chapter 1

God Calls Us to Love

This is My commandment, that you love one another as I have loved you.

—JOHN 15:12

I WAS STANDING NEAR THE PIT, the place believed to have been the lions' den into which King Darius the Mede threw the prophet Daniel more than twenty-five hundred years ago. Charged with disloyalty to the king because he prayed to his sovereign God, Daniel was thrown into the pit to be devoured by ferocious lions. But Daniel was in God's favor, and the Lord protected him so that he was not harmed.

As a small child I had dreamed of visiting ancient Babylon someday. I wanted to gaze into that pit where Daniel had once stood, surrounded by lions. I also wanted to see where other exciting stories had taken place in that historic city of Bible times. These were only dreams of my childhood that I never imagined would come true. Then, more than a half-century later I was among the ruins of the city of Babylon. It was thrilling to realize that King Nebuchadnezzar's chariots had once rolled on the excavated streets where I walked.

On the walls of buildings bordering those ancient streets were images of dragons, molded in bold relief on fired-brick building blocks. Some of the glazed tiles that had once adorned the famous Ishtar Gate were still there. Continuing on from the remaining walls of one building to the next, I searched for evidence of Babylon's famous Hanging Gardens, but nothing remained. What my Iraqi guide identified as "the pit, the lions' den" was still there. For a moment I imagined that in that darkened pit there might still be hungry lions crouching in the shadows, growling, flashing their sharp teeth, ready to devour their prey.

Entering the reconstructed banquet hall of Nebuchadnezzar's palace, I stood before the high wall said to have been where God caused a hand to appear and to write the words, "MENE, MENE, TEKEL, UPHARSIN"—words warning Belshazzar, successor to King Nebuchadnezzar, that the days of his kingdom were numbered. The Bible says, "That very night Belshazzar, king of the Chaldeans, was slain" (Daniel 5:30). Perhaps you are wondering why I was in the ancient city of Babylon. I will answer that question later in this chapter.

I first heard about Daniel and the city of Babylon when my mother read Bible stories to me. Later, I heard the stories told all over again in Sunday school. Our family went to church on Sunday mornings and evenings and sometimes for mid-week services. My father was an elder in our church, and I admired him very much and wanted to be just like him. At age twelve I accepted Jesus Christ as my Lord and Savior.

After years and years in school I was finally handed my diploma as a Doctor of Medicine. Sylvia and I were married the day before medical school graduation, and we were ready to find our place together in the world.

Faithfulness in church attendance became an important part of our life together. When we were blessed with the births of two sons and a daughter, we read to them those same Bible stories we had heard as small children—one of them about Daniel in the lions' den.

Hearing the Call

Neurosurgical residency training seemed to go on forever, but finally, at age thirty-four, I was a fully trained neurosurgeon, ready to begin living life in the fast lane. Every day in my practice meant long hours in the operating room—all too often becoming an all-night marathon. The work was hard and demanding, but I felt good about my life as a neurosurgeon. I was helping people who were sick and injured, and I felt this was what God wanted me to do.

Approaching my fiftieth birthday, a certain "sameness" came to my life and my practice. Sylvia and I were very happy. We enjoyed the rewards of success and didn't mind living our lives in overdrive, but something was missing. We both felt "a still, small voice" was asking for our attention. We knew it was the Lord speaking to us, not in an audible voice but through His Holy Spirit. We felt He was saying, "I have blessed you in so many ways, but what have you done for *Me* in the living of your lives?"

We began to search for answers to the question we believed God was asking us. As we were doing so, I heard about an urgent need for a neurosurgeon in Peshawar, Pakistan, to help treat the wounded people fleeing over the Kyber Pass to escape the war in Afghanistan. I telephoned the number for the Lady Reading Hospital in Peshawar as many as thirty-five times but was never able to make a connection. Perhaps this was God's way of saying, "No, this is not the place I want you to go."

Then early one morning in 1984, as Sylvia and I were having a second cup of coffee before my busy day in the operating room, I was channel surfing, looking for the news. "Quick, go back," Sylvia said. "I think its Billy Graham!" I returned to the program in question, but it wasn't Billy Graham; it was a young man who looked and sounded like Billy Graham. Then the name "Franklin Graham" appeared on the television screen. This young man was further identified as the eldest son of Dr. Billy Graham and president of Samaritan's Purse, a Christian international relief organization. Franklin Graham shared that he had not always followed in his well-known father's footsteps. He then told how, one night when he was twenty-two years old, he had gotten down on his knees, confessed his sin, and given his life to the Lord.

As we watched, Franklin showed photographs he had taken at Tenwek, a Christian mission hospital in Kenya. They showed three or four patients in the same hospital bed, and more on the floor underneath. Then he looked directly into the television camera and said, "We need Christian doctors who will go to mission hospitals like this one to bring medical treatment to patients who will otherwise not receive care." In that moment, Sylvia and I felt we heard God's voice speaking to us. Almost in unison we said, "Yes, we'll go!"

I called the number on the screen. Becky Williams, the placement director at World Medical Mission, the medical arm of Samaritan's Purse, listened as I told her I was a neurosurgeon. I told her that my family and I wanted to volunteer to go to the mission hospital in Kenya, the one Franklin Graham had just been describing. After a long moment of silence she questioned whether I would be able to perform any neurosurgery at Tenwek Hospital. She seemed to politely imply, "I don't know if we can use a brain surgeon in a bush hospital in Africa. You see, what we need are real doctors!" That was a really big lesson in humility for a somewhat full-of-himself neurosurgeon from Southern California! Still, Becky Williams was very encouraging in terms of possible opportunities for short-term missions service somewhere else in the future, and she sent an application for each member of our family.

Going with God's Plan

After a few weeks Becky called us and asked if I would be willing to work short-term in South Korea. This would be at a large hospital where a visiting professor was needed to lead the training program in neurosurgery while the hospital's neurosurgery department chief came to the U.S. for more training. There was only one problem: we didn't want to go to South Korea! The plan our family had in mind was to go to Tenwek Hospital in Kenya. Still, we prayed about it, and then I called Becky and said, "Yes, we'll go!"

I could never have imagined that God's plan for my life would also call me to do work for Him in *North* Korea thirteen years later.

At Presbyterian Medical Center in Chonju, South Korea, I worked as a visiting professor of neurosurgery. Sylvia worked in hospital administration and taught English to Korean hospital employees. Our teenage children worked in various capacities in the hospital. Even though we had gone to Presbyterian Medical Center to be "givers," we found that we were the "receivers," and our lives were changed.

Sometime after we returned from South Korea, Becky called to say that Samaritan's Purse had received good reports concerning our work there. Then she said, "They are really desperate for doctors at Tenwek, that bush hospital in Kenya, located fifty miles from the nearest town. If you are willing to do general medicine, general surgery, and deliver babies, along with whatever neurosurgery you might be able to do, perhaps we can use you there."

I didn't say it but I thought, *Fine, I can do that. After all, I used to be a "real" doctor!*

Along with eighteen duffel bags and suitcases filled with medical equipment and supplies, our family of five flew to London and then to Nairobi, Kenya. From there we were flown in a Cessna 206 missionary aircraft to the mission hospital at Tenwek, where we landed on a grassy landing strip.

My first neurosurgical patient at Tenwek Hospital was a twenty-six-year-old Kipsigis tribesman named Stanley Cheborge. Stanley had lost his right leg to bone cancer several years before. Now he was experiencing pain in his back and his remaining leg. When I operated on Stanley's spine and found it was riddled with cancer, I knew he would not have long to live. I found time to talk with Stanley each day as I monitored his postoperative recovery and his response to impending death, and I was captivated by his strong Christian faith. Whenever I had a few minutes between operations on other patients, I found myself going to Stanley's hospital room to listen to more of his compelling story.

Stanley told me he had once been a very aggressive, mean-spirited, ruthless, conniving person who lived only to please himself. When illness and personal loss entered his life, he had lost his leg at Tenwek Hospital, but he had found Jesus Christ and accepted Him as Lord and Savior, and his life had been completely changed. Through my close friendship with Stanley Cheborge I came to realize that God works in mysterious ways. He used a one-legged African man who lived in a mud-walled, mud-floored, grass-roofed hut to lead a neurosurgeon from Southern California to make a midcareer change and redirect how he was going to live the rest of his life.

After those first mission trips to South Korea and Kenya, Sylvia and I continued to serve short-term assignments in Christian mission hospitals. But in the years that followed, things began to change in the world. Increasingly, assignments through Samaritan's Purse were not only to Christian mission hospitals, but also to places where wars were being fought.

After the fall of Communism, Christian relief work through Samaritan's Purse took us and many other volunteers to Somalia, Rwanda, the former Soviet Union, Bosnia, Kosovo, the Congo, Central and South America, and to other places of war, conflict, natural disaster, and great need around the world. Over and over again as we have done the Lord's work, we have seen Him provide help that has made an important difference in the lives of those who are hurting. Ordinary people, just like you and me, have responded to God's call to bring help to the sick, the suffering, the wounded, and the seemingly forgotten people in our world.

As Jesus demonstrated during His earthly ministry, God's plan calls us to bring help, healing, and hope to people *one person at a time*. One person who is willing to show God's love and share the gospel with others who are in need. One person like Franklin Graham, who was once a self-described rebel, but now leads both Sam-aritan's Purse and the Billy Graham Evangelistic Association. And one person like Stanley Cheborge, an African tribesman who lived only to please himself until he accepted Jesus Christ as Lord and Savior and experienced new birth.

What then is the irresistible yet undeniable truth that is common to the lives of Franklin Graham and Stanley Cheborge? I believe it is that each of these men has been able to hear God's voice! If you and I were to listen, what will we hear Him saying to us? At any moment He may be saying different things to each one of us, but the Bible tells us the command to *love* Him and to *love* our neighbors as we love ourselves will be prominent in His words for us. Jesus said, "God so *loved* the world . . ." (John 3:16; italics mine).

The prophet Daniel lived more than five hundred years before the birth of Christ, and he loved God totally and completely. God honored Daniel's love, obedience, and faithfulness to Him by using him to bring help to the people taken captive in Judah and exiled in Babylon. With God's protection and help, Daniel served King Nebuchadnezzar, King Belshazzar, King Darius the Mede, and King Cyrus of Persia. God kept Daniel free from harm even when Darius the Mede cast him into the lions' den. Throughout a lifetime that extended into his nineties, Daniel was given the power to serve, and to survive, in high places because his love for God never wavered.

In the book of Daniel we read that King Nebuchadnezzar loved only himself and had overwhelming personal pride. God warned Nebuchadnezzar of the perils of pride when He spoke to him through a disturbing dream that only Daniel could interpret. God warned Nebuchadnezzar that he would live for seven years away from other people in the presence of wild animals in order that he might be humbled. After seven years, when Nebuchadnezzar would come to acknowledge that heaven rules, his kingdom would be restored. However, in spite of God's warning, Nebuchadnezzar remained prideful and God carried out his sentence. Seven years later Nebuchadnezzar was humbled, and as he raised his eyes toward heaven his sanity was restored. Then he praised God, saying, "Now I, Nebuchadnezzar, praise and extol and honor the King of heaven, all of whose works are truth, and His ways justice. And those who walk in pride He is able to put down" (Daniel 4:37).

Visiting Babylon

One of the greatest tyrants of modern history is Saddam Hussein, former president of Iraq. Hussein has lived as a man of pride with a heart of evil, even envisioning himself as the Nebuchadnezzar of our time. Saddam Hussein and his regime are responsible for much of the danger facing our world today. Because of Hussein's evil ambitions, a reported one million Iranian soldiers and an estimated eight hundred thousand Iraqi soldiers lost their lives during the eight-year war with Iran, initiated by Hussein. He is believed to have caused the deaths of thousands, if not millions more of his own people, and he brought terrible hardships and suffering upon the rest of the Iraqi people, qualifying himself as one of the most evil rulers in history.

It was because of the suffering of the Iraqi people that Franklin Graham sent our Samaritan's Purse team to Baghdad in the early summer of 2000. Our mission was to see if medical relief could be given to the Iraqi people without violating the restriction guidelines imposed by the UN embargo on that country.

Our team of four flew to Amman, Jordan, where we met with the Iraqi ambassador to Jordan. He showed us public health records that listed appalling statistics concerning the healthcare status of children in Iraq. Among children under five, deaths from diarrhea were up 1300 percent from March 1989 to March 1999. Respiratory illness deaths were up 1380 percent, and deaths from malnutrition were up 3500 percent. In spite of these healthcare needs, Saddam Hussein had just finished building his seventeenth lavish royal palace. He was also in the process of building the largest mosque in the world while spending large sums of money to rebuild the ancient city of Babylon for his own glory.

In 5:00 a.m. darkness, we loaded our gear into a large four-wheel-drive sports utility vehicle that had been dispatched to take us to Baghdad, and then we began our journey toward the Jordanian border with Iraq. Three and one-half hours later we arrived at the border. After clearing our credentials with the

Jordanian officials, our driver proceeded toward a twenty-foot-high concrete structure displaying the likeness of Saddam Hussein, his smiling face welcoming us to Iraq.

At the Iraqi border station, we were told to get out of our vehicle. We watched as customs officials disappeared with our SUV in a cloud of dust, taking it to some undisclosed destination for inspection. In the small, one-story customs and immigration building we surrendered our passports and were told to sit down in a large room with oriental carpets on the floor and smiling photographs of Saddam Hussein on the walls. After waiting for more than an hour, the Iraqi officials handed us our passports and escorted us to our vehicle, which had just been returned following a thorough inspection. We continued our journey toward Baghdad, traveling at speeds of eighty-five to ninety miles an hour.

For another six hours we were driven across the Iraqi desert on a remarkably fine national highway built by the government of Saddam Hussein during the years when money from the sale of oil was plentiful. As the sun was beginning to set behind us in the West, we arrived at a bridge crossing the Euphrates River. Our driver stopped for a few minutes to allow us to stretch our legs. It was exciting to see this historic river and to realize that thousands of years before, Abraham and his family must have walked alongside it as they made their journey from the land of Ur to the land promised to them by God.

Just before dark we arrived at the front entrance of the Al-Rashid Hotel in central Baghdad, located not far from the main presidential palace. On the floor of the marble entry to the hotel was a mosaic of former president George Herbert Walker Bush, making it necessary for anyone entering the hotel to step on President Bush's likeness, representing one of the greatest personal insults to someone according to Iraqi customs. Below his image were the words "Bush is criminal," in English and Arabic.

The following morning, we were driven to the government building housing the Ministry of Health, where we had a forty-five-minute meeting with the assistant director of international health for Iraq. He told us the nation's water supply, sewer system, and basic infrastructure had deteriorated to crisis levels, but he blamed this on the UN embargo and not on the regime of Saddam Hussein. Next, we met for more than an hour with the Iraqi minister of health. He spoke passionately of the suffering of the Iraqi people, especially the children, placing the blame for their suffering on the UN embargo against his country as well as long-term effects of degraded uranium left behind from the shelling by U.S. forces in Desert Storm.

Following this high-level meeting was a visit to Baghdad Children's Hospital. Before I could get out of our vehicle, a man thrust his seven-year-old daughter through the open car window into my lap. I climbed out of the vehicle and the little girl's father took her back from me, holding her in his arms as he and the little girl's mother pleaded for help in Arabic.

The little girl was very pale and had clotted blood in her left nostril. I felt sure she had leukemia. When one of the hospital doctors joined us, he confirmed this diagnosis and told me medication for the child's treatment was not available in Iraq. Then he said, "It is because of the degraded uranium left over from shells used by the United States during Desert Storm that this little girl and many others are sick and suffering." Clearly the agenda of Saddam Hussein's followers was to convince our Samaritan's Purse team members that the healthcare crisis in Iraq was the result of the UN embargo.

Each day as I worked in Baghdad's hospitals I was asked to examine large numbers of sick and deformed Iraqi children. It was obvious the Ministry of Health had notified parents of my presence in Baghdad, instructing them to bring their sick children to be seen. Almost all of these children were afflicted by some neurological problem for which no help could be given; a number had been born mentally defective, likely because their parents were first cousins. Other children were sick or disabled as a result of various infectious diseases, leukemia, tumors, or other conditions for which modern, state-of-the-art medical care was no longer available in Iraq. At one time the quality of medical care delivery in Iraq was reportedly unequaled in the Middle East, but under the rule of Saddam Hussein this was no longer true.

On one unforgettable morning in one of the Baghdad hospitals the examination room seemed especially hot, the air heavy due to high humidity. As usual, long lines of deformed, sick, and suffering little children accompanied by their anxious parents filled the hallway, waiting to be seen. These parents were seeking a miracle they believed I might perform because I was from America.

After examining the first few children, an Iraqi mother dressed in a black chador covering all but her saddened face sat down in the chair in front of me. In her outstretched arms lay her comatose child, a little boy of about four. He was totally limp and unresponsive. She reminded me of Michelangelo's sculpture *The Pieta,* depicting the mother of Jesus, sitting, holding the lifeless body of her dead son. The Iraqi mother anxiously began to speak in Arabic, explaining with impassioned words how several months earlier her little boy had fallen ill with a high fever, experienced convulsions, and lapsed into a deep coma. My examination of the little boy found he had evidence of severe brain damage, and I knew nothing could be done. Turning to the young Iraqi doctor assigned as my interpreter, I said, "Please tell the mother there is nothing I can do to help. Please tell her that she should continue to love and care for her little boy, and that she should pray to God, asking Him to bring healing to her son's body."

Hearing my words translated, the mother began to cry. Tears streamed down her cheeks, and she reached forward, pushing her motionless little boy into my arms. Between sobs and cries of painful anguish she seemed to be pleading with me in Arabic. I knew she was asking for help, and there was nonc I could give. The interpreter was silent for a long moment and then he said, "The mother is saying, 'Please take my son back with you to America. I will give him to you, and he will be yours. I am prepared to give him to you, if only you will take him with you to America where you can perform a miracle and restore him to health.'" I wanted to cry as I looked at this comatose child and into the tear-filled eyes of his grieving mother. My heart was broken.

What are we to do, if we are going to make a difference in our dangerous world? We begin with *love*—bringing the love of Jesus Christ to our world. Mark 12:30–31 tells us we are to first "love the Lord our God with all our heart, with all our soul, and with all our mind," and then we are to, "Love our neighbors, as we love ourselves."

With the successful conclusion of the war to remove Saddam Hussein and his evil regime from power in Iraq, we have witnessed evil through the medium of television news. We have seen mobs gather with clenched fists and shouts of hatred, not expressions of love for God and for other people. The forces of evil are at work around the world, and the need to replace this evil with hope and love through coming to know Jesus Christ is urgent. Today as never before, the church of Jesus Christ is positioned to do the work God has called us to do. A network of Christian workers reaches around the world with ability to bring compassionate help and God's love to people in need. By bringing a cup of cool water to a person who is thirsty, a piece of bread to one who is hungry, and medical care to someone who is sick or injured, we then earn the right to share the gospel of Jesus Christ.

On our final night in Baghdad, seven of the Iraqi physicians we had worked with hosted a farewell dinner for us. Words of friendship were exchanged as the Iraqi doctors spoke of their appreciation for our having come to assist them in caring for sick patients. They spoke of their admiration for us as caring physicians and expressed amazement that we had come to Iraq to help the Iraqi people. At the end of the meal, the most senior surgeon said, "I am afraid you will not be able to leave tomorrow." For a moment I wondered if he was telling us we were to become political prisoners! But then he added, "We have warm feelings of friendship for you, we do not feel it safe for you to travel across the desert tomorrow because of the predicted sandstorms."

Fortunately, the weather cleared overnight. As we prepared to leave Baghdad the following morning, a high-level official in the Department of Health asked to speak privately with me. Extending his hand, he said, "I have come to admire and respect you very much as I have observed the compassionate way in which you have treated patients, families, and others while in my country." As we were shaking hands, I felt him press something into mine. Having the forethought to simply close my hand and place the small object in my pocket, I avoided creating awareness by other Iraqi officials of the transaction.

Once safely out of Baghdad I took the object from my pocket and found it was a tightly folded piece of paper. Written on it in pencil were these words: "If it is possible I would like to leave Iraq and become a Good Samaritan, like you. During your time here you have shown compassion and brought love to those whose lives you have touched." Reading these words, I felt God's purpose for sending our Samaritan's Purse team to Iraq had been fulfilled.

Iraq has now been liberated, and humanitarian relief is being brought to the people who have suffered so long under evil, oppressive rule. Saddam Hussein, who thought of himself as the Nebuchadnezzar of our time, has been captured. The statues and monuments he had constructed to bring honor and glory to himself have been torn down. Saddam Hussein's oppressive regime is history. The marble mosaic meant to show former president Bush as a criminal to be stepped on has been broken into small pieces and removed. God remains the same yesterday, today, and forever, and He is calling us to show His love in our hostile, suffering, and dangerous world.

Jesus warned his disciples this would be difficult. Perhaps as never before in history, the dangers facing those who lift up the name Jesus seem to be increasing among people hostile to Him here at home and in other countries. Still, people are suffering, and the followers of Jesus Christ have been called to step forward, reaching out to them in His name. Our job is to make a difference.

Before you turn the page, ask yourself these questions:

- Do I want to make a difference by responding to God's call to love the world?
- Have I taken time to be quiet and listen so I can hear God's voice?
- How will I answer the question, "What have you done for Me, in the living of your life?"

chapter 2

God Sends Us to Love

By this all will know that you are My disciples, if you have love for one another.

—JOHN 13:35

ONLY THE ROAR of the Russian Ilyushin airliner's engines broke the silence as the vintage aircraft made its final approach to the landing strip of North Korea's Pyongyang International Airport. You know the reason for my mission there—to find ways for Samaritan's Purse to show God's love through bringing help to people who were sick, hungry, and in need.

Every seat in the airplane was filled. I looked around the cabin, wondering who the other passengers might be and why they were on this flight to Pyongyang. Some were North Koreans, as evidenced by the small, colored enamel emblems they wore on their jackets, positioned directly over their hearts. The emblems bore the likeness of President Kim Il Sung, who died in 1994 but has been named by the government, "President for Eternity."

After touching down we taxied for a long period of time on a seemingly endless runway before coming to a stop thirty yards from the small terminal with the name *Pyongyang* displayed in large letters. The only other visible aircraft were four aging Russian airliners parked nearby with pods covering their silent jet engines. Several dozen soldiers in military uniform stood near the entrance to the arrivals area, but otherwise there was no sign of activity at this international airport terminal. Only a gently blowing breeze broke the unusual silence as I deplaned and boarded the bus to transport us the short distance to the darkened airport terminal.

North Korea was the last place I wanted to be at that time. My heart was thousands of miles away in Detroit, Michigan, where my daughter and her premature baby were in a hospital. But for now I knew I needed to focus on what God had called me to do in the Democratic People's Republic of Korea.

Waiting patiently to clear customs, I thought again of the reports that an estimated two million people had already starved to death in North Korea and of fears that many more might die in the months ahead. I could still remember all too well the terrible war fought between the United States and North Korea more than fifty years ago. Following the cease-fire signed in 1953, North Korea virtually disappeared from the radar screen as far as the world was concerned. When Communism collapsed in Eastern Europe the economy failed, and North Korea became a country of hungry people experiencing great need. Once again Franklin Graham and Samaritan's Purse had the opportunity to bring God's love and humanitarian assistance to the people of this hermit kingdom. This was why I had come to the DPRK.

MISPLACED RELIANCE

After clearing passport control and customs, North Korean officials drove our small Christian delegation through a military checkpoint guarded by uniformed soldiers. They appeared thin and expressionless as they stood with 1950s-era weapons. Our vehicle continued toward Pyongyang on a beautiful, wide highway almost devoid of other vehicles. Large numbers of people, many in military uniform, walked on well-worn footpaths along each side of the highway. It seemed strange that no one appeared to be talking with anyone else.

Near the city, the highway widened into an imposing boulevard lined with Russian-style apartment buildings. Along the route were large, concrete structures displaying the smiling face of their late president Kim Il Sung. Two tall structures as we entered the city caused me to think once again of King Nebuchadnezzar and the ancient city of Babylon. The first was a huge, bronze statue of the late president Kim Il Sung, symbolizing the importance of a human being whom people in the DPRK look upon as a deity. The second very imposing structure was the Juche Tower, a beautiful monument of granite and marble built to symbolize the national philosophy of the DPRK called Juche, meaning "self-reliance." President Kim Il Sung espoused Juche as the official philosophy of the North Korean people, but this is not in keeping with God's plan for us to be reliant upon Him.

North Korean government officials blame the terrible floods in 1994 and 1995, which were followed by two years of severe drought, for no longer being able to produce enough food to feed their twenty-two and one-half million people. Also, for more than fifty years the North Korean media have unleashed bellicose words of hatred aimed at the United States, blaming our government for the war of 1950–53 and for the separation that continues between the North and the South. Hatred toward the U.S. is preached to the Korean people from early childhood. What they do not acknowledge is a failed political and economic system, further weakened by very heavy expenditures for their military.

Thankfully, in America we do not hear words of hatred or threats of attack against the DPRK. The purpose of this book is not to proclaim hatred toward anyone; this book has been written in obedience to God's greatest commandment, to *love*. We are to *love* God, who first loved us, and then, as Jesus said, we are to love our neighbors as we love ourselves.

It must be our prayer that the leadership and the people of the DPRK will turn away from feelings of blame and hatred toward the U.S. and other countries and that they will allow God's love to come in. In so doing the door will be opened for them to receive humanitarian assistance.

A Big Problem and a Simple Cure

During that first visit to North Korea on behalf of Samaritan's Purse in 1997, my focus was on the healthcare needs of the people. The tuberculosis (TB) pandemic stood out as a problem. I met with six doctors and several hospital administrators at a TB hospital in Pyongyang. The hospital director made a long presentation detailing the history of the hospital, the great accomplishments of its staff, and the great numbers of TB patients being treated there. Yet I did not see any sign of patients in the hospital. The hallways seemed dark, even in daylight hours, and I was told there was no electric power available. In the hospital laboratory there was only one microscope and one glass-fronted supply cabinet that was virtually empty. The sink had a constantly dripping tap.

In the x-ray department, a thin, gray-haired man in a white coat greeted me. He identified himself as the chief radiologist and proudly showed me the hospital's only x-ray machine, pointing to four decal "awards" stuck to it. He told me he had received these awards for keeping the x-ray machine clean and tidy. Then he added, "This x-ray machine has not been operational for the past four years because there has been no electric power in the hospital to run it, and we have not had x-ray film available for a longer time than that."

The hospital director explained, "Tuberculosis has long been endemic in North Korea, but in 1970 the late president Kim Il Sung in his great wisdom announced a five-year plan to eradicate TB." Before this proclamation, people were periodically screened for TB using x-ray machines positioned in van-type vehicles. When the five-year period ended in 1975, their president had announced, "TB has been eradicated"; therefore, no further testing was done. As a result of this proclamation, TB continued to spread, finally reaching crisis levels during the time of widespread famine. Healthcare services deteriorated during the early part of the 1990s.

During a visit to a TB rest home, located far out in the country side, I saw a woman of about sixty who was coughing repeatedly. The rest home physician told me that her name was Mrs. Kim and that she had been in the same room with three other women, all with active tuberculosis, for the past thirty-six years because no medical treatment had been available.

I was told that patients placed in North Korean TB rest homes are separated from their families and friends and are considered to no longer exist. It was sad to hear this, knowing that with a six-month TB treatment program 85 percent of these people could be cured. With surgery and more intensive medical treatment most of the remaining patients could also be cured. Furthermore, the approximate cost for medications necessary for this treatment would be only thirty-eight dollars per patient.

One of the rest home doctors pointed to some trees with small, red berries outside the long, low-roofed buildings in which patients were housed. He proudly told me he was treating TB patients with the red berries, saying, "I have nothing else with which to treat my patients. So I give them berries from the trees in the hope the berries may be effective in treating the tuberculosis making my patients sick."

I wondered how it could be possible in our twenty-first-century world to have a country so isolated from the rest of the world that two million people could starve to death while food was plentiful in other countries. To have a society where an estimated two and one-half million people suffer with tuberculosis although most could be treated and cured at a very low cost. A country where even basic medical care is nonexistent.

God's provision came in the form of a Christian donor and his family who heard of this plight and made treatment medication available. Because of their generosity Mrs. Kim and an estimated fifteen thousand other North Koreans have been treated, no longer suffer with tuberculosis, and have been returned to their homes and families. The Samaritan's Purse TB screening, diagnosis, and treatment program has shown the love of Jesus Christ to people in the DPRK and has brought medical care to them.

Through humanitarian relief and showing God's love, we can pray that relations between the DPRK and other nations will improve and that the dangerous confrontations that have existed in the past will be resolved. Our prayers are that in God's timing reunification between South and North Korea will take place, peace will prevail, and Pyongyang will one day again be called "The Jerusalem of the East." God has done similar work in recent history.

Several years ago, I was with Franklin Graham and others from Samaritan's Purse in Vietnam. On our first morning in Hanoi, a government representative entered the room, took his seat next to Franklin, and said, "Welcome to our country. You can travel to the north, to the south, to the east and to the west and you will not find one person—man, woman, or child—who will mistreat you, be rude to you, or in any way be unfriendly toward you. Things have not always been good between your country and ours, but that is the past. We live in the present and look to the future. We welcome you to our country as friends."

Hearing these words I thought, *May it be our prayer that officials in the DPRK will also come to know this same willingness to forget past hostilities and differences and respond to the invitation by the United States, South Korea, and other countries to join in a spirit of friendship. What a difference it will make for the DPRK to move away from deep hostility and hatred so the people who now suffer there may receive food and humanitarian assistance and once again know God and His love.*

Sharing God's Love from Home

Like the prophet Daniel, Mary Damron is humble before God and has chosen to live her life in obedience to Him and share His love with others. Born into poverty in the hills of West Virginia, Mary felt destined to remain there. She believed her entire life would be spent living in the same house with the leaking roof that she and her family call home, seldom venturing more than a few miles away from the place of her birth. But then Mary heard God's voice and responded to His call to reach out to the forgotten children of the world with simple gifts showing the love of Jesus Christ.

Here's how Mary tells her story:

> I was raised in heartache, abuse, and extreme poverty. My father was an alcoholic. My mother left my eight brothers and sisters and me when I was ten years old. When I

became a Christian, God gave me a burden for helping other people, especially during their time of pain and suffering. He gave me a special heart for children. Perhaps because of the physical and the emotional pain I experienced in my own childhood, He has enabled me to identify with them. I understand how physical circumstances can cause someone to feel ashamed, worthless, and less than human.

I still live in the place of my birth and youth, in the heart of the Appalachian Mountains of West Virginia. My husband and I have been married for thirty years, and we have been blessed with three children and three grandchildren.

In 1994 things were probably better for me than at any time in my life. Still, there was a problem. I was beginning to feel a heavy burden for the children in war-torn Bosnia and in other African countries where I knew many people were suffering and dying because of famine. I grieved with this burden for four months and felt sure God had placed this concern before me. One evening, as I was on my face in prayer, asking God to do something, I suddenly felt He was answering me, saying, "You do something!"

A few minutes later I switched on our television set and saw Franklin Graham telling about Operation Christmas Child. It's this wonderful idea of simply taking an empty shoebox and filling it with small items for a child in need somewhere in the world. I could see this was something that could be done by virtually anyone, no matter what age and how rich or poor. Franklin explained how these filled shoeboxes could be collected, taken to Samaritan's Purse for the Operation Christmas Child program, and then sent to needy children in countries around the world.

I thought, *Wow, Lord, this is something I can do, and it will bring smiles and happiness to little children who are in need, while showing the love of Jesus at the same time.* I got some empty shoeboxes and started filling them right away, and from that day in 1994, I haven't stopped! Then God gave me an idea. Why should only I fill shoeboxes with gifts, when I could get other people to do the same and end up with even more gifts for children? I got in our old pickup truck and started going to our neighbors, to gas stations, 7-11 stores, churches, schools, and everywhere else I could think of. And I didn't just do this in Ikes Fork; I went to all of the hollers and valleys and towns in the area, asking people to "fill an empty shoebox for God."

Before long, I had collected over twelve hundred filled shoeboxes, and I felt ready to go meet this Rev. Franklin Graham. I loaded all of the shoeboxes in the back of a borrowed twenty-ton truck, and early on Thanksgiving Day morning, I headed for Samaritan's Purse in Boone, North Carolina.

My life has never been the same since that evening in 1994 when I finally took time to be still and listen, so that I could hear what God was saying to me and to find what He was asking me to do! In fact, my life has become so full since I have started serving the Lord that I would never want it to be like it used to be again.

Because of the number of shoeboxes I had collected back in 1994, Franklin asked me if I would like to go with him and his team from Samaritan's Purse to distribute the gifts. I went with them to Croatia that year, and the following year I was part of the small team Franklin took right into Sarajevo to hand out shoeboxes while there was still fighting going on in Bosnia.

SHOEBOXES AND LOVE

I was with Mary, Franklin, and others from Samaritan's Purse on that hair-raising journey to Sarajevo in 1995. The way the Lord worked through this little mountain woman was powerfully portrayed on that hazardous trip as God led her in lifting up the children of Sarajevo, replacing their sadness and despair with excitement, joy, and happiness through the Operation Christmas Child program.

Our team of twelve flew from Zagreb in Croatia to the seaside city of Split, on the Adriatic Coast near Dubrovnik. In two rented vans, we drove to the Bosnian border and then continued into former Yugoslavia to Mostar, an ancient city severely damaged by shelling during the war of ethnic cleansing. After leaving Mostar, we made the gentle climb toward the mountain range that separated us from the besieged city of Sarajevo in Bosnia and Herzegovina.

Darkness was beginning to fall by the time we arrived at the United Nations military checkpoint that was positioned at the entry point to the mountain pass that led to Sarajevo. Two large army tanks guarded the pass. After showing the UN soldiers our credentials, Franklin told them we were en route to Sarajevo. The UN soldier in charge said, "Sir, it isn't safe for you to go beyond this point. Proceeding will require you to drive through a mountain pass that is held by the Serbian Army. It would be especially dangerous for you to proceed with darkness falling. I am sure you understand the additional danger for the female members of your group."

Franklin asked if there was an alternative route, and the UN soldier said the only other way would be to take the narrow, winding mountain road that passed over the top of Mount Igman. It was already growing dark, and snow was beginning to fall, but after a brief discussion and a time in prayer, our team members agreed that we should continue our journey. We had come this far to deliver shoebox gifts to the children in Sarajevo, and with God's help this was what we felt we had to do.

At first the three-hour drive over the mountain presented no real problem, but then the snow started to fall more heavily, and the night turned into pitch darkness. The farther we drove, the more narrow and hazardous the road became.

There were long periods of silence in our vehicle as we climbed higher and higher up the mountainside. Near the top of the mountain we could see the bright headlights of a large truck approaching from the other direction. It was an eighteen-wheeler that seemed to occupy the entire width of the narrow mountain road. Its driver moved as far toward the side of the road as possible and stopped to allow us to pass. As our van inched along, hugging the snow-covered mountainside, we slid against the truck. Our team climbed out, leaving Franklin at the wheel. Working in heavily falling snow, we were able to push our van away from the truck enough to move past it. Then we continued down the mountainside toward Sarajevo.

Reaching the lower elevations, snow turned to freezing rain and heavy fog. Visibility dropped to about fifty feet as we finally came to level ground on the valley floor. We had no idea where we were, and we took turns praying for God's leading. It was a humbling moment as we each realized how totally dependent we were upon God for His protection. Driving onward in pouring rain, we bounced from one mortar-shell hole to another. We assumed we were somewhere near Sarajevo but couldn't be sure.

The only sounds were the rain pelting on the van's metal roof and the rhythmic swishing of the windshield wipers. Finally, Dennis Agajanian said, "Guys, we have arrived in hell!"

We saw a sandbagged bunker about fifty yards ahead. A UN soldier in helmet and flak jacket emerged with an automatic weapon at the ready and began walking toward us. After checking our credentials, the UN soldier said to Franklin, "Sir, you are in a no man's land between the battle lines of opposing military forces, and it is not safe for you to be here. Please proceed forward while carefully staying on the road in order to avoid land mines. I will call ahead to the next sentry post to alert them that you are coming. We will try to guide you into Sarajevo."

In the pouring rain and dense fog, we proceeded to the next sentry post and then to the next, finally seeing ruins of apartment buildings that I remembered from an earlier visit were near Sarajevo's airport. We crossed a bridge, then made a right turn, and found ourselves driving down Sarajevo's "sniper alley."

There was very little light in the large, cold, and drafty ten-story hotel building in which we were to spend the next two nights. Many of the hotel's windows were covered with plastic sheeting because shelling had blown away the glass. Throughout the night we heard occasional small-arms fire.

The following morning we visited hospitals, giving Operation Christmas Child shoebox gifts to sick and injured children. Franklin asked me to visit Sarajevo's large teaching hospital, and to take Mike MacIntosh, senior pastor of Horizon Christian Fellowship in San Diego, California, with me.

As Mike and I talked with one of the young female doctors at Sarajevo Hospital, she told us how she had worked there as a surgeon throughout the entire war:

> Day after day over these past several years, I have operated on one patient after another, and many of them have died because of their terrible wounds of war. In doing my work as a surgeon I have operated all day, all night, all the next day, and then that night. After operating on even more of the wounded on the third day, then I have been off-duty for the short hours of that third night.
>
> Because of the terrible evil I have seen, and because there has been no hope in my life or theirs, on my night of rest I have turned to drink in order to try to numb my troubled mind. I sit there and drink, and then I cry. Then I drink some more and cry more until my brain becomes numbed enough that I fall into a deep sleep. In the early morning hours I hear the nurses calling my name, telling me my time of rest is finished, and there are more patients who need my care. I have no hope. In these times, nobody in Bosnia has any hope!

Mike MacIntosh asked this troubled young doctor if we could pray with her. Mike and I bowed our heads, and he prayed a beautiful prayer, asking God to bring hope into the life of this young lady, and into the lives of the people of Sarajevo. As Mike said, "Amen," we opened our eyes and found the doctor sitting with her eyes wide open. Then she said, "I am sorry, but I close my eyes with no one, not even you, because there is no person I feel I can trust."

That evening, our Samaritan's Purse team went to a military armory building where two hundred or more children had been assembled and were waiting for us. It was odd to see so many children sitting quietly and without emotion. Then Mary Damron did something magical. She climbed up on the stage, took a microphone in her hand, and introduced herself to the children, pointing out that she wasn't very much bigger than most of them. Mary explained how she had once lived under very difficult circumstances but then came to experience happiness through knowing a loving God. She told the children we had come to Sarajevo to share His love, bringing gifts for the children.

Tommy Coomes began to play his guitar and to sing songs of praise. The children started to move to the rhythm of the music. Smiles began to appear on their faces. Mary, small in stature but seeming to have the volume of a full gospel choir, began to sing. Several kids stood up and started clapping, leading Mary to hand off the microphone and start clapping to the beat of the music.

Dennis Agajanian's massive presence appeared from behind the curtain, and the children were in awe as they looked up and saw him, shadowed by his large-brimmed Stetson cowboy hat, towering over a guitar. Grammy Award-winning country and bluegrass performers Ricky Skaggs and Sharon White Skaggs joined Dennis from the other side of the stage. Music filled the large room, and the place went wild! It seemed every child in the auditorium was now clapping and jumping up and down, keeping time to the music. Mary jumped off the stage and started a line dance around the room. One child after another joined in until all two hundred or more kids were forming one long chain of energy, moving around the large armory floor dancing, laughing, shouting, and singing.

At first the parents sat looking on, but soon they were on their feet clapping and keeping time to the music as well. Wide smiles, long absent from their faces, exposed decaying and missing teeth, but no one cared. Every person was a child again, and happiness filled the room.

There was laughter, dancing, and deafening noise, and it was a wonderful, never-to-be-forgotten moment. The fear and the evil that had cast a pall over the city of Sarajevo for more than three years of war had suddenly been partially swept away by the love of Jesus Christ. At least in these moments in a crowded room, hope and happiness and love had been restored. The one person who had been used by the Lord to start this amazing transformation was a five-foot-tall mountain woman from Ikes Fork, West Virginia. A single solitary child of God who had grown up poor, had suffered much, but had then been made incredibly rich in spirit through coming to know a loving God, through His Son Jesus Christ.

When everyone was out of energy and out of breath, the music and the dancing stopped. Mary took the microphone again and asked all the children to sit down. Then she told the story of a little baby who was born in a stable to a humble and very poor mother and her carpenter husband nearly two thousand years ago. This baby, born of a virgin mother, was God's Son, and He was sent into the world in this way to show us His love and the way we are to live. You could have heard a pin drop! All those children were hearing a story more exciting and more wonderful than they had ever heard before—and they wanted to hear more.

Then our team members began to present brightly colored Operation Christmas Child shoebox gifts to all those children, giving a shoebox to each child, one at a time. After every child in the room had a shoebox, Mary counted, "One . . . two . . . three!" On the count of three every child opened his or her shoebox. Happiness and excitement erupted all over again, and there was the feeling of wonderful chaos in the room. These little children had probably never received a present just for them. Some were so excited at seeing the beautiful toys, gloves, caps, books, flashlights, and hard candy in their shoebox gifts they replaced the lid, waiting to share their gift with other family and friends once they returned home. Most of the children just sat on the floor and began to play with their toys, put on their caps and gloves, or to eat their hard candy.

In more than one hundred countries around the world, the love of Jesus Christ is being shown in a very simple way through the miracle of a shoebox filled with gifts for a little child. In those same one hundred or more countries, Samaritan's Purse is at work showing God's love and bringing help to those who are down-and-out and feel they have no hope.

God has called us to love our neighbors as we love ourselves. He has called us to show His love by reaching out to those in need. He is asking us to make a difference in our world.

Before you turn the page, ask yourself these questions:

- Do I love God enough to be faithful and obedient in serving Him?
- Am I prepared to say, "Yes, Lord, I'll go; send me"?
- Do I stand humbly enough before God to allow Him to use me in His service?

chapter 3

In Jesus' Name, We Are to Love

By this we know love, because He laid down His life for us. And we also ought to lay down our lives for the brethren. But whoever has this world's good, and sees his brother in need, and shuts up his heart from him, how does the love of God abide in him?

—1 JOHN 3:16–17

HAVE YOU EVER MET PEOPLE with so much love in their hearts for those around them that they seem to glow with that love as it is radiated from their faces? I met a person like that on March 8, 1992.

It was a Missions Sunday at the Community Presbyterian Church in Palm Desert, California. That morning I had brought the message about medical missions work in developing countries. The text I had used focused upon the abundant ways we have been blessed and God's calling to share from our abundance with others.

As I stood outside the sanctuary after the service, the first person out of the church rushed up to me and said, "Hi, I'm Barb Peters, and the Lord really spoke to me through your message. Here is a check for Samaritan's Purse to use in showing the love of Jesus and bringing help to those people in Africa you talked about. I'm a real estate agent and I have to go to work now, because what I believe God is calling me to do is make money to give to the church to help people who are in need. Bye!" The check was very generous.

Barb became a friend, and several years later she went with Sylvia and me to Kenya in East Africa on a mission trip. What she experienced there greatly impacted her life, and she wrote about it, focusing on her time at a place called Londiani.

> I saw abject poverty, suffering, and starvation. I saw the sick, two or three in each hospital bed and more on the floor underneath since there were not enough beds to accommodate the numbers of sick people who were in need of help. I smelled the sickening odor of disease and death. And I saw children wandering the streets, helpless and alone. Seeing these things brought cultural and psychological shock to me that changed my life, causing me never to be the same again.

JOSÉ CARRERAS—THE INITIAL MOTIVATOR

My journey to Africa started in a most unusual way, and it was with my introduction to opera and the person of José Carreras. His music thrilled me, and his autobiography told of his battle to overcome leukemia, and how he had become so self-absorbed in his professional career that he had forgotten to place God first. Then he responded to God's call for service to others in His name. He wrote, "Love is the life-giving force; a person's success should be measured not by what he or she achieves, but by what he or she has done to bring help to other human beings."[1] After reading his words, I realized I had become a captive of the same materialism Mr. Carreras was referring to and that my good intentions were being smothered by pursuit of things of this world.

From childhood, I wanted to become a doctor so I could serve God by working with people who were underprivileged. In my fifties, I sold my home and moved into a humble abode to afford to attend university and go to medical school. Actually, had my dream been realized, I would probably have been the oldest graduating doctor ever! Still, I believed that even if I was too old for medical school I might be able to get a doctorate in science and work in a mission hospital as a lab technician.

While working a full-time job in real estate sales, I studied hard and was able to make it through the first year. I wrote to my friend Dr. Mel Cheatham, to tell him of my studies and desire to serve in the mission field. I remember writing in my letter to him, "In about six years I will be ready to serve in a mission hospital."

He replied, "How about now? You have two masters' degrees already and a background in teaching, and someone like you is badly needed at a mission school in Londiani, Kenya. The teachers there need the expertise you have to train them, and they need it now."

Now? Kenya? I gulped.

Being a person who is used to the finer things in life, who takes germs very seriously, I had visions of tribal warfare, genocide, natives on the rampage, AIDS, malaria, the Ebola virus, and all sorts of other things. Still, I managed enough courage to ask the next question: "Where is this Londiani? Look what you have got me into, Mr. Carreras!"

I found Londiani was a small village in western Kenya. Another Christian missionary was already there and had started the school. She was now building a medical clinic and dreamed of starting a small hospital.

When I announced, "I am going to the jungle this summer to work as a missionary," my grown children were not encouraging. "You know, you're losing it, Mother"; "I'm proud of you, Mom, but can't you do something nice and safe that is a little bit closer to home than East Africa?" "I really don't care what Mr. Carreras said in his book, I don't want you to die."

I finally blurted out, "I tried to teach you how to live, and now I am going to teach you how to die." (I knew this reply sounded very pious, but actually I was rather proud of myself for being able to come up with it so quickly.)

The Journey Begins

First, there were inoculations to get. As my doctor plunged the hypodermic needle into my posterior, I said to God under my breath, "I hope You are taking note of this!" Then I collected educational materials, begged medical supplies from physicians in my area, and soon had three seventy-pound duffel bags filled to overflowing. My clothes and other personal belongings were packed into a roll-aboard bag. And then there was the big, bright yellow CD player. When I agreed to take it with me to Africa, I had no idea how big this music box was going to be.

The CD player was indeed large, but it played the music of Mr. Carreras so beautifully and I wanted to share it with the people in Londiani. I placed the player in a large canvas bag, along with my entire collection of Jose Carreras operatic and sacred music. The British Airways employee who checked me in for the flight to London looked at me sternly and said, "That bag is twelve inches too long, six inches too wide, and twenty pounds overweight. It doesn't qualify as a carry-on! You are already at your maximum allowed limit on weight for checked luggage!"

I responded, "I need everything in my bags when I arrive in Kenya so I can play José Carreras music for the natives." The man stared at me for a very long moment, then said, "Go! *Just go!*"

I thought I was prepared for what I would experience in Africa. But I was wrong. In Rwanda, for instance, I saw almost every building in the capital city of Kigali pockmarked with bullets or partially destroyed by mortar shells, evidence of the rage of one tribe of men and women against another. I saw widows who were alone with no way to cope in a male-dominated society. And my heart was broken by the numbers of orphaned children with nowhere to go. Then in Londiani, I too felt alone after the other members of our Samaritan's Purse team journeyed on to other mission hospitals.

Londiani is not in the jungle, but in a large valley at approximately seven thousand feet elevation. It was the rainy season, or monsoon season is more like it. The people in the area lived in mud-walled, mud-floored huts with grass roofs. Many were dressed in rags and walked barefoot. I never saw anyone who was fat or old. The people were softspoken, would have been appalled if anyone raised a voice in anger or disrespect, and laughed easily and often. They adored and hovered over their children. These were a gentle, beautiful people, and I fell in love with them immediately.

God and José

My job was to observe the progress of the medical clinic and to hold training programs for national teachers. I did my best, but with the rain, the cold, the constant mud, and the difficulties I encountered in communicating with teachers, I began to feel very alone and discouraged. I prayed, *What on earth am I doing here, Lord? I am in this remote, disease-infested area, cold, wet, sick, and apparently useless. I am probably the saddest example of a missionary you ever sent to do your work.*

I decided to try one more time to be a good servant for the Lord. With a heavy heart I began my long, lonely walk down the muddy road to the school. The rain was splashing down, and with each step I felt I was sinking deeper into the mud. I was struggling to carry my books, my teaching materials, my umbrella and my "Big Yellow Submarine CD player." I felt so miserable and unhappy that I decided to turn on a little José Carreras music, from the opera *Andre Chenier.*

Then a strange thing happened. Men, women, little children, big children, people I didn't even know appeared from nowhere. They came from the fields, from the trees, and out of their mud huts and started following me! First one and then another asked, "What is that music, and where is it coming from?"

Turning up the volume, I said, "It is an opera by Carreras. It is one of my favorite operas. The music is coming from a CD—a compact disk, inside my CD player."

Then the questions started coming from the whole crowd. "What is an opera?" "What is a CD?" "What is a Carreras?" "What is a CD player?"

By the time I reached the school grounds with my CD player still blaring, children had rushed up to me, surrounded me, and almost crushed me in their eagerness to hear, to see, and to touch. A crowd of adults and children were all around me and in that moment I felt like the most popular person in the whole world.

Inside the school building, I told them the story of José Carreras. I told them about opera and about the world beyond Londiani. When the rain had stopped, we all went outside and sat on the wet grass under a clear blue sky, and I played the CD of Jose Carreras singing sacred music. I believe in that moment we could all feel God's presence among us, and the children, the teachers, the adults, everyone, including me, listened with tears streaming down our faces. In that moment I knew why I was there—why God had brought me twelve thousand miles from home to a place called Londiani. He had brought me there as His messenger to share His love, and to tell everyone about His Son, Jesus Christ. He was using me to bring His Word and beauty and love into the lives of these wonderful African people.

God was using the Giant Yellow Submarine CD player I had lugged all the way from California, and the music of José Carreras, a man who believes deeply in Him, to provide a needed breakthrough for me. Now I was in demand. I used my CD player and the music it provided as an instrument through which to teach. In biology classes I taught the students about the disease that had threatened the life of Mr. Carreras, and how God had led doctors to use the miracles of modern medicine to save his life.

In science classes, I explained the nature of electricity and the use of batteries to store energy for use when needed. In music classes, I was able to teach vocabulary and word meaning through playing songs from *Sound of Music* and other popular songs of our time. As I explained the plots of some of the operas, the students found the stories to be very amusing, and we were able to laugh and bond together. Most important of all, through the music I was able to share with students, teachers, and parents the story of Jesus and how He loved the little children. I told them how they could be born again through coming to know Him as Lord and Savior. I shared the fact that God is love and that He loves every one of His children and wants us to experience this life with abundance and then to receive His greatest gift: living with Him in heaven forever.

I never again had to walk alone down that long, muddy road. Loving people, both young and old, always surrounded me. We hugged each other and laughed, talked, and sang together as we walked side by side as Christian friends, listening to the Big Yellow Submarine CD player turned up to full volume! Each night a different teacher would take the CD player home to listen to Puccini, Verdi, Bernstein, Tschaikovsky, and others. Their huts were always filled with friends and neighbors who came to hear the music.

When I left Londiani there were hugs and kisses, smiles and tears. I left empty-handed. The Big Yellow Submarine CD player and my entire favorite CD collection, along with my books, all of my clothes other than what I was wearing, and the rest of my money stayed there. And part of my heart stayed there too. The people of Londiani planted a tree in my honor, the highest commendation they can pay to a friend. This caused me to look to the heavens beyond the bright, blue sky that seems to stretch forever above the savanna of Londiani, and to thank God for the way He blessed my life in bringing me to that place to do His work.

Maybe someday one of the children I was privileged to teach at Londiani will have an opportunity to go to a university. Perhaps God will use him or her to be the one to discover the cure for cancer or to find a treatment for AIDS. Maybe out of Londiani will emerge the next great opera singer, and he or she will sing praises to our mighty God who loves us so much. But

> the one thing I am absolutely sure about is that if the love God has for us can be transformed into love between all of the people of this world, it will cease to be a dangerous place in which to live.

If we are to make a difference in our dangerous world, the Bible tells us we must have the kind of abundant love seen in Barbara Peters's story.

We live in a world of contrasts, but none is greater than the difference that exists between those who have love for their neighbors and those who have hatred toward them.

The Magnificent Seven

What a contrast between shouting words of death from militant people who hate and the tender, compassionate love from a gentle grandmother named Barbara Peters, who seeks to help others. And what a contrast between people who harbor enough hatred to blow up innocent people and those with love in their hearts like Gene Edmonds, P. D. Roller, Gene Middleton, James Parrish, Billy Tarlton, Charlie Simpson, and T. C. Carter. Each of these men was in his fifties or sixties, had a compassionate heart, and felt called by the Lord to show His love by giving to others in their time of need. Others nicknamed this group of men "The Magnificent Seven," but they consider themselves to be only humble servants of the Lord Jesus Christ.

It was August 1999, and Sylvia and I were in the city of Gjakova, Kosovo, sharing a rented Muslim house with these seven men. We had all traveled thousands of miles from home to bring help. The mission of The Magnificent Seven was to build roofs for homes that had been bombed and burned by Serbian soldiers who threw incendiary grenades into them. These seven men worked ten- to twelve-hour days in their effort to accomplish their task in time to provide protection for Muslim families facing the approaching harsh cold of winter. Early each morning these men left our rented house for the one-hour drive to the place in the mountains where they would work. At the end of each day they returned, covered with dust, their clothes soaked with perspiration, their muscles aching, and their bodies sunburned, but with excitement as they told of the experiences of that day.

Just before finishing their tour of volunteer mission service, Gene, Billy, Charlie, James, P. D., T. C., and Gene came back to our rented house one evening with a special burden on their hearts. As we ate baked beans and bread the men said to Sylvia and me, "Those little kids out there at that house we are putting a roof on hardly have a thing to eat. In their village, all but the old men have either been killed off by the Serbs or have disappeared, maybe taken to prison. Those little kids need some milk to drink. We found a milk cow today that we can buy for them, and we are going back to that farmer tomorrow to get it."

It was amazing, challenging, uplifting, and a real blessing to be able to share times of prayer each morning and then devotions each evening with these seven men who were indeed "The Magnificent Seven," but for God's glory and not their own. They truly had love in their hearts and they demonstrated what people even beyond the prime years of their lives can do in His service, if they are willing to say, "Yes, Lord, I'll go; send me." There is tremendous power in God's love. The stories of those who have chosen to love and to give to others in His name provide inspiration for us all.

Christmas: Christian/Jewish Style

A lady I will call Shoshana knows all about the love of Jesus Christ. She is a Jewish lady in her late sixties, living in Israel. Her neighbor is a young Christian lady I will name Amanda who recently graduated from medical school in Israel and who, while there, married a young Jewish man I will refer to as Aaron. When Amanda and Aaron fell in love and wanted to get married, they found it would be impossible in Israel since unequal marriages—marriages between Jews and non-Jews—are forbidden by Jewish law. Therefore, Amanda and Aaron had to go to one of the Greek islands to get married. After returning to their studies in Israel the newly wedded couple encountered great animosity, especially from traditional Jews. Shoshana knew Amanda was not Jewish, but she remained friendly and was never rude or judgmental concerning the marriage. In fact she was very generous in baking treats and bringing them to Amanda and Aaron's apartment.

As Christmas of 2002 drew near, Amanda decided to invite some of her friends for a party to celebrate Christmas Eve, and her husband Aaron was in agreement with this. Amanda's family had sent some Christmas decorations, Christmas music, and a very small Christmas tree from America so she decided to decorate the apartment. Before the party, Shoshana arrived at the door with some baked goods. When she saw Amanda and Aaron's apartment so beautifully decorated she exclaimed, "Oh how wonderful! I so miss celebrating Christmas!"

Amanda was stunned. She was very surprised to hear a Jewish person in Israel say what she heard Shoshana say. Then Shoshana explained her remarks by telling a story she had kept locked up inside her heart for many years.

When I was a very little girl, my family and I lived in Romania. With the start of World War II, Hitler began to round up the Jews, and my parents were under no illusion about what was going to happen to them and to us as their children. They confided their fears to friends who were Christian, and this family said they would take me and my siblings into their home and pretend we were their children. I remember so well my parents saying good-bye to us through their tears, and the tears I shed as my mother and father walked away to accept the fate that awaited them. The Christian family became parents to us children and raised us as their own. In the years that followed, we always celebrated Christmas and other holidays as did other Christian families.

Later, after I had grown up, I came to Israel, and since I am Jewish by birth I became a religious Jew, accepting Judaism as my faith. But I have always continued to carry in my heart the love of Jesus Christ that my "Christian parents" taught me all those many years ago. And through my friendship with you, Amanda and Aaron, I have been able to show His love to you, and to give things to you as an expression of His love.

FINDING GOD'S LOVE IN THE RIGHT PLACES

Leilani Vail also knows God's love now. She thought she knew all about His love and the love we are to have for others. Then she and her husband, Floyd, signed on to make a trip around the world with Sylvia and me, visiting mission hospitals and schools in several countries. Leilani likes to tell how God changed her life through what she saw and felt on that journey—about experiences that were so powerful and so wonderful that she hardly knows where to begin in describing them.

> As we traveled from one country to another, God showered us with His love, leading us to feel a peace and a joy we had never known before. We experienced God's love through the friendship of others on our team. Thirteen people with diverse backgrounds came on this arduous journey to seek their own special way for making a difference in the lives of others.
>
> I felt God's love through selfless people Floyd and I had never known before but will never forget. Teachers were committed to bringing knowledge to barefoot children in ragged clothes, studying in classrooms with dirt floors and no windows. Doctors and nurses labored to bring healing to people who were desperately ill and sometimes dying. I saw God's love in the smile of a little girl who had an enormous brain cyst that hung through her face, displacing one of her eyes. Pearl Winterbourne, an eighty-year-old lady living on a mountaintop in the Congo bush, teaches God's Word and started schools and a hospital in that remote location to bring help to people of a Pygmy tribe. God's love was in the eyes of a man who became a paraplegic after he stepped on a land mine in Vietnam. Now he moved about through the dirt in a wheelchair, helping his beautiful blonde-haired wife care for their ten adopted children, seven of them disabled in some way. But making this middle-aged couple truly remarkable were the two hundred young children who also called them Mom and Dad, because they were the directors at Good Shepherd's Fold Orphanage in

Uganda—caring for children who had lost their parents to AIDS.

Through seeing God's love in the lives of countless saintly people in a dozen different countries during that trip around the world, I came to realize you don't need to be brilliant or scholarly or a gifted surgeon or a teacher to do His work. You only need to be willing to open your heart to others, so that you may be used by God to show His love. People may never experience His love unless someone like you tells them about Him and leads them to know how to receive His love.

In our dangerous world today, there is a special urgency for us to show our love to others. This is made greater because of the more than one billion people in the world whose professed religious beliefs advocate violence and terrorist acts against others. This unquestionable urgency exists because of extremists in many countries, of various ethnic backgrounds, cultures, and religions, but who have in common the unspeakable evil, hatred, and desire to bring death and destruction to others who believe differently. But the Bible tells us none of what these people hold in their hearts and minds can equal or overcome God's love and the love of His Son, Jesus Christ.

Before you turn the page, ask yourself these questions:

- Do I really love my neighbor as I love myself?
- Am I experiencing the abundant joy of sharing God's love with others?
- Do I realize the power of God's love as I share it with others?

PART 2

The Privilege to Give

chapter 4

We Have Been Called to Give

But a certain Samaritan, as he journeyed, came where he was. And when he saw him, he had compassion. So he went to him and bandaged his wounds, pouring on oil and wine; and he set him on his own animal, brought him to an inn, and took care of him.

—LUKE 10:33–34

CAROLINE had just turned three when her world became dangerous. On July 25, 1940, she was proudly riding her new tricycle on the sidewalk in front of her home in Plymouth, England, when the bombs began to fall. The German Luftwaffe unleashed terror from the skies on frightened, innocent people, and the Battle of Britain in World War II had begun.

Caroline McNeill Love was blessed to grow up in a Christian home. For her upper-middle-class family, church attendance was a very important part of life. Her mother taught Sunday school; her father, a Christian physician, put his faith in action through care of the sick and wounded through the nearly five years of World War II. He had already survived many dangers while serving as an army medical officer in Mesopotamia and Gallipoli during World War I.

Voice for the Voiceless

Caroline's faith grew progressively during the war, and in her early teens she began to feel called to give her life in service to others. As a student nurse she met and married a young physician, Dr. Murray Cox. They were blessed with two sons and a daughter and planned to go to the mission field. After qualifying as a nurse, however, Caroline fell ill with tuberculosis and was hospitalized for six months. Their dream was placed on hold.

Meanwhile, God's calling to help others led Caroline Cox to work among the socially disadvantaged in the poorest areas of East London and to a career as a sociologist and social activist. In her heart she still longed to be a missionary, but her compassionate caring for others did not go unnoticed, in part because she was so vocal in speaking out on behalf of disadvantaged people. Caroline felt a special burden to become the voice for those with no effective voice of their own.

On December 7, 1982, Caroline Cox received a telephone call asking her to come the next day to Number Ten Downing Street to meet with Prime Minister Margaret Thatcher. The prime minister asked if Caroline would accept a life peerage. Caroline was astounded by this invitation to become a member of the House of Lords but happily accepted the appointment. In a short time she was given the title Baroness Cox of Queensbury.

Perhaps, as happened with Lady Caroline Cox, you are sensing that the Lord is calling you to give to others who are suffering in our dangerous world. You can do this, as she did, by sharing with them your time, your talents, and your resources. But, you may be wondering, *What can someone like me do, that will make a difference in a dangerous world?*

The example of Baroness Cox of Queensbury has answers to this question. God instilled in her a loving heart and a compassionate spirit. He gave her boundless energy, a brilliant mind, and an unusual ability to communicate with others. Her place of residence and work is London, England, but her mission field extends to the far corners of the world. She often goes to places where others would fear to go, doing so in order to bring humanitarian assistance to people in need and to show God's love to them. Through God's leading she has become a voice for the voiceless, giving help to the helpless wherever they may be in the world.

Caroline Cox's stories captivate those who hear them, touching their hearts and inspiring many to say, "Yes, Lord, I'll go; send me. You have so abundantly given to me that I feel called to give, for Your glory, to others."

If you have been blessed to hear her speak, you have almost certainly heard her say something like this:

> Come with me for a moment, as we fly into one of the forbidden areas of the Sudan. The military regime doesn't want us in no-go areas, and they threaten to blow us out of the sky if they get the chance. But we have brave pilots who are willing to trust God for protection and fly us to forbidden airstrips.
>
> Deep inside Southern Sudan, all we can see from horizon to horizon is smoke, like back in England when we burn the stubble after the harvest. But this smoke is from villages that are burning. As our little plane touches down, people come up to us with tears running down their

cheeks. They say, "We are so happy to see you. We thought the world had forgotten us." They tell us how a few days ago, Islamic government forces two thousand strong attacked the area, rounding up the villagers and slaughtering them. We see the bodies of these innocent people, laying all around us, rotting in the heat. The people say to us, "Come footing with us as we walk through the bush, and you will see what the Islamic soldiers have done." We go footing with them for twenty kilometers and see nothing but the remains of a complete scorched-earth policy: burnt cattle, burnt homes, and the bodies of women and children who tried to flee but had not been able to escape.

We arrive at another township just after a raid. The Christian pastor there tells us he had been away and when he returned he found they had killed his mother and his brother-in-law, had burned the little church and all the Bibles, and had taken his sister as a slave. He said, "You know we Christians here in Southern Sudan are so alone. We are trying to hold a frontier of Christendom, but we have been ignored by the whole world and feel so forgotten. You are the only Christians who have even visited us for many years.

We must remember this pastor in our prayers and then when we return, we can tell him and his people we not only want them, we cherish them, and they have not been forgotten. Should the day come when they must endure their martyrdom, we will be worthy of their sacrifices for our faith.

The love and compassion that Baroness Cox feels in her heart for those who have been forgotten with no one to speak for them, flows from her lips as she tells of the places where God has called her to go. Through another story, she invites us to experience with her what she has seen and heard:

> Come with me in these next few moments to another airstrip in an area where the Muslim raiders attack and kill the men and take the women into slavery. They take the children away from their homes, knowing they can bring them up as Muslims. The Muslim slave owners abuse the women sexually, changing the genetic makeup of the children they will bear.
>
> Sit with me under a mango tree as I talk with little Deng, who has just been bought back from slave traders. He is only ten, and his little face is very sad because after being a slave in captivity for over two years he is now home and has found that his parents have been killed in a raid. He has just learned he is an orphan.
>
> We go to another area around the oil fields where the people are being ethnically cleansed by the Islamic regime as it exploits the oil. At yet another airstrip we find again that the earth has been burned to blackness and the people rush to our airplane shouting, "Thank God you have come. Please join us as we go footing."
>
> Again we walk through twenty kilometers of scorched-earth devastation. Six thousand homes, eleven churches, seven mosques, and a hospital are gone. But suddenly, we hear the sound of celebration, of people singing! "What is all this merriment about?" we asked. And they exclaim, "It's wonderful! Praise the Lord! One of our pastors has just returned from footing through the bush. He has just baptized eleven thousand new Christians and established

seven new churches!" So the Holy Spirit is at work. Our faith is growing here in the Sudan even under tremendous persecution.

Now come to worship under the spreading, circular branches of a beautiful tamarind tree. The people have arranged logs to make seats and this is their "cathedral." Listen with me to the words of a fellow Christian worker, exiled because he criticized the Muslim regime, as he speaks to his people saying things that are written in my heart. These are his words:

> Here we are, in this most beautiful cathedral, not built with human hands, but by nature and by God, filled with the people of God, and especially with his children. You people here in Sudan still smile, in spite of suffering, persecution, and slavery. Your smiles put us to shame. Many of you feel embarrassed because of your nakedness. But I say to you, don't be embarrassed because *true nakedness* is to be without love. Be clothed in love—that is, Christianity. Show your love to those who do not know our Lord and His love. We must leave you, but we will not forget you, and we will continue to pray for you.

Here Caroline Cox typically pauses in her story, drops her head, and for a few moments seems very far away. Looking up again she resumes, "Here is the challenge to all of us. Prayer without deeds is dead, as love without action is dead! Our prayers and our love must be in action . . . I came, I saw, I heard, I touched, and I am enriched!"

Baroness Cox's heart is joined with the needs of the "voiceless people" in Africa, especially those who suffer in the Sudan. But her calling from God extends beyond Africa, as far as Burma and to the historic Armenian land of Nagorno-Karabakh. She shares stories from these faraway places such as this one:

> The voices of the ethnic minorities packed in the jungles of eastern Burma are not heard, and the people are suffering severely. They are rounded up and used as forced labor with conditions so harsh that many perish. Even little children, as soon as they can carry weights of a few kilograms, are used. Old people have to carry thirty kilograms of heavy weapons each day, passing through mine fields as they do so, and many are annihilated. Come with me to a village that has just been attacked by Burmese soldiers. The countryside is like the Sudan, with everything destroyed. Entering the village we see the remains of burned huts, still smoldering. Soldiers have run through the village, just ahead of us, indiscriminately shooting civilians left behind.
>
> In one hut left standing we found a lovely lady called Ma Su. She was shot in the raid, her husband was killed, and her house was burnt. She lost everything. I ask her what her feelings are for the soldier who shot her. Her reply is very simple: "I love him because it says in the Bible we are to love our enemies. So of course I love him. He is my brother." What a miracle of grace her words are, of Christ's transforming love! She is an example of the grace abounding in the persecuted church.
>
> What a privilege for us to be with forgotten people like these, even if it is only to give the encouragement of a brief visit to the place they call home, where they struggle to survive.

Giving in Somalia

As Caroline Cox certainly knows, we live in a world of hatred and evil—a world made especially dangerous because of international terrorism. It is believed the roots of what we now know as Al-Qaeda were already at work against U.S. forces in Somalia more than ten years ago, when Osama bin Laden was beginning his evil jihad. On March 10, 1993, I was there as part of a Samaritan's Purse international relief team during the terrible war between fiercely rival clans loyal to rival warlords.

I had heard of Dr. Dick Bransford, but in Somalia I was privileged to meet him for the first time. His name was legendary among Christian medical missionaries in East Africa, and I looked forward to working with him. Several days after Sylvia and I arrived in Mogadishu, Dick asked me to accompany him to see some patients in a remote village some twenty miles west of the city. On this typically hot, humid day the wind was blowing across Mogadishu and its surrounding sandy desert, depositing fine dust and grit in our eyes.

We had instructed Ali, our Somali driver, not to slow down through the danger-filled streets of Mogadishu. Anyone we met in the rubble-strewn streets was a potential thief waiting for any opportunity to reach into passing vehicles and steal whatever they could, even sunglasses off our faces. There was no recognized government in Somalia, and things as basic as ball point pens were treasured as bartering items to obtain food.

As we passed mound after mound of freshly dug sand, the nauseating smell from superficially buried victims of the tribal war was overpowering. The tragedy that would later be called "Black Hawk Down" had not yet taken place, but the potential for a deadly attack against U.S. forces was obvious. Without question,

Mogadishu was a dangerous place for nongovernment organizations like Samaritan's Purse that were trying to bring help to a people in desperate need.

I turned to look out the back of the vehicle and found myself staring into the dark, steely eyes of Abdulahi, the younger of the two Somali guards hired to protect us, both armed with assault weapons. The evil in his eyes glared back at me, and I wondered what terrible things he had seen and done. I knew he had grenades on his person and even though his job was to protect us, it was at my head that his AK-47 rifle was aimed. I stared at Abdulahi for a long moment, and apparently realizing my discomfort in looking into the barrel of his weapon, he smiled faintly and lowered it. Feeling somewhat relieved I asked, "Abdulahi, how old are you?"

"I am seventeen," he answered.

The village of Afgoy, where we were to set up a medical clinic that morning, is about twenty miles west of Mogadishu. Four UN soldiers in a UN Humvee followed our Land Rover for our protection. They told us an Irish nurse had been fatally shot in the head by a Somali sniper while traveling on this same road just two weeks before.

Arriving at our destination, our Samaritan's Purse team unloaded footlockers filled with medical supplies and hung a tarpaulin between the Land Rover and a mud building to provide some protection from the hot sun. Within minutes, long lines of Somali men, women, and children gathered, anxious to receive the basic medical care we had come to give.

After about two hours, the oppressive heat had become almost unbearable, and our medications and supplies were running low. Then several young Somali men came into the village brandishing long knives and threatening trouble. Fearing a possible hostile attack, the UN soldiers who were protecting us suggested we load up our gear and leave as quickly as possible.

Along the Afgoy Road back toward Mogadishu, the UN Humvee again followed our four-wheel drive Land Rover. Two of the four UN soldiers were standing in the open roof with automatic weapons at the ready.

Our driver, Clarence, from our Samaritan's Purse Canada office, suddenly slammed on the brakes, saying, "There are guys with guns ahead!" The Humvee veered off the road to the left and gave chase as the armed men fled into the underbrush. Lacking our protective escort, we were frightened as we watched more Somalis gather on the road about a hundred yards ahead of us. Dick Bransford broke the silence. "We are sitting ducks here, and those guys blocking the road ahead look dangerous. Give it full throttle, Clarence!"

Clarence did "give it full throttle," and the UN personnel carrier reappeared behind us in a cloud of dust following close behind as we roared ahead, directly toward the crowd. The Somalis quickly scattered to the sides of the road. Ignoring standard military convoy speed of forty-five miles per hour, Clarence drove us back to Magadishu as quickly as possible.

During those days with Dick Bransford in Somalia, I came to know him as one of the most compassionate, caring, giving people I had ever met. Since 1993, our paths have crossed many times and we have worked together in other short-term assignments. The story of Dick and his wife, Millie, is an amazing one, and I want to share a synopsis of it with you.

RESPONDING TO GOD'S CALL

Have you ever dreamed of being or doing something and then had to accept the fact that you just didn't have what it would take to realize your dream? That was Dick Bransford's experience.

Throughout junior high and high school Dick longed to be a good athlete, but somehow the skill just wasn't there. The hours he wanted to spend at football or basketball practice were filled with study because Dick didn't consider himself a very good student, and he knew the importance of earning good grades. After graduation from high school, Dick couldn't afford to go away to a major university, so for his first two years he lived at home and attended nearby Compton College. "I had a good time at Compton and began to dream of the day I could marry the girl I had been dating for three and a half years. However, she married my best friend, instead of me," he said.

Is Dick Bransford's story beginning to sound like Charlie Brown in *Peanuts?* Well, perhaps so if his story ended here, but in his walk with the Lord, Dick felt God was calling him to become a doctor. Believing there was no way he would ever be accepted by a medical school, he decided to "go for the gold" by applying to the prestigious Johns Hopkins University School of Medicine in Baltimore, Maryland. He could not have been more surprised when he was in fact accepted there! Feeling humble and "out of my class," Dick studied hard at Johns Hopkins.

During one spring break he attended an InterVarsity Christian Fellowship conference which led him to go to an InterVarsity missionary camp. En route to the camp he shared a ride with a beautiful young Christian girl named Millie. This proved to be a shared ride made in heaven, and a year later Millie and Dick were married.

Life was tough at first for the Bransfords. They had little money, medical school debts were growing, and study and work commitments meant Millie and Dick saw too little of each other. Dick offered to drop out of medical school, but Millie insisted he continue his studies. A year later, with the support of a scholarship,

Dick and Millie flew to Nairobi, Kenya, where he worked for a time at Kijabe Mission Hospital. This experience defined the direction for their future.

When Dick returned to his medical school studies, it was with a renewed purpose. After he graduated from Johns Hopkins School of Medicine as Richard Bransford, MD, the Bransfords knew God was calling them to be medical missionaries; but first Dick had to complete a four-year residency in general surgery followed by two years of active duty as a United States Air Force surgeon. By this time Millie had given birth to two sons and to a daughter. Something truly remarkable about people like Dick and Millie Bransford is their willingness to study, work, and prepare so hard, for so many years, in order to give their lives away in service to others.

Following discharge from the air force, there was still more for the Bransfords to do to prepare them for the Lord's service. With their three children they went to Switzerland to learn French and then to Belgium to study tropical medicine, which is necessary for medical missionaries in Zaire. When their assignment came through, it was not to Zaire, but to the Comoro Islands where 99.9 percent of the people are Muslim. Two significant events occurred there. First was the birth of their twins, Jonathan and Susie; the second was that Dick became very ill with tick typhus. The family returned to Kijabe Mission Hospital near Nairobi, where Dick could recover his health and gain back the thirty-five pounds he had lost. Kijabe became their home.

At Kijabe Mission Hospital, Dick was amazed at the number of children he saw with orthopedic abnormalities, often congenital in nature but sometimes due to joint infections or diseases like tuberculosis and polio. Knowing there were no missionary doctors in Kenya trained to do this corrective surgery, Dr. Dick Bransford took time from his general surgery practice to learn the operative procedures necessary to help these children. News of Dr. Bransford's newly learned surgical skill traveled fast. The volume of patients soon far exceeded the capabilities of Kijabe Hospital. So he designed and personally raised the money to build a children's rehabilitation hospital at Kijabe, naming it after his daughter Bethany.

Dick Bransford didn't stop at being a missionary doctor, operating on endless numbers of crippled children, administering Bethany Children's Rehabilitation Center, and going to outlying areas around Nairobi to operate surgical clinics. The needs of sick, suffering, hurting, and oppressed people in other parts of Africa were so great that Dick felt God had called him to make a difference in the lives of people who suffered in other African countries, as well.

A few months after being with Dick Bransford in Somalia over ten years ago, Sylvia and I made the journey into Rwanda with him and with his daughter Bethany. Since then Dick has responded to God's call for service in the Congo and many times in the war-torn Southern Sudan. It seems that wherever there are people in need, Dick Bransford responds to God's call to help with His work. And Dick does so with the deepest possible humility, giving the Lord credit for everything.

Millie Bransford works just as hard in her role of homemaker, mother, and missionary at Kijabe. Raising their five wonderful, God-loving, God-fearing children while living under the often-difficult conditions of life in rural Kenya would seem a big enough challenge to most people, but along the way Dick and Millie adopted two Kenyan children, Joshua Moses and Philip James.

How is it possible that people like Dick and Millie Bransford can do this work halfway around the world from home? A commitment of love and a willingness to give such as this can be explained only through a complete, unquestioning love for God.

Lady Caroline Cox of England and Dr. Richard Bransford of Santa Ana, California, both work tirelessly in their calling to make a difference.

In a dangerous world, both are humble, giving the praise for the work they do to their sovereign God. Even at significant risk to their own lives, they remain committed to serving others.

God has called you and me to love our neighbors as we love ourselves. He has called you and me to give from our abundance in service to others. The time for us to do this is now! The need is urgent! The opportunities are many! Each one of us can make a difference. All we need to do is to respond to God's call, saying, "Yes, Lord, I'll go; send me. Lead me to do that one unique and special thing You have planned just for me."

Before you turn the page, ask yourself these questions:

- What is God calling me to do with my life?
- What God-given gift do I have that I can give to help others?
- What can I do to better prepare myself for helping others?

chapter 5

With God's Help, We Are Able to Give

So I say to you, ask, and it will be given to you; seek, and you will find; knock, and it will be opened to you. For everyone who asks receives, and he who seeks finds, and to him who knocks it will be opened.

—LUKE 11:9–10

TANYA WAS A BEAUTIFUL, exceptionally bright, twenty-two-year-old lady, ten thousand miles from home. She missed her mother, father, and younger brother so much that she would often awaken in the night and cry. Committing her life to helping others had brought her to this place, so far from home. Yet gaining acceptance to medical school represented fulfillment of her greatest dream, and she knew it was an answer to prayer. If only she could be studying medicine in her native Russia, instead of ten thousand miles away in Israel, but this was not possible.

It was Friday morning in Jerusalem, the busiest time of the week as people made final preparations for the Shabbat. It would begin at two o'clock in the afternoon and continue until sundown on Saturday. The waiting area for the emergency room of Shaare'i Zedek Hospital was crowded with patients and their anxious family members and friends. In each examination cubicle bed there was a patient either undergoing evaluation of some complaint or already receiving emergency treatment.

The largest marketplace in Jerusalem was only a few blocks away. Enveloped in the crowd of Friday morning shoppers who were making their way toward the entrance to the marketplace was a woman who appeared to be very pregnant. Carefully observing each person who approached the market were Israeli soldiers armed with M-16 rifles.

Suddenly, the woman who appeared so pregnant pushed other people out of her way and ran toward the entrance to the market. Reaching inside her coat she pulled a wire, activating the hidden dynamite pack tied about her torso and causing it to detonate. A massive, ear-piercing explosion followed. The woman was killed immediately, and body parts along with other items of debris were sent flying through the air like deadly missiles. Many who were near the woman fell injured, stunned, and bleeding. Chaos erupted as security guards and soldiers rushed to the bloody scene. Scores of terrified shoppers ran in all directions, seeking that place of safety they knew in their hearts no longer existed. As the smoke cleared, two young Chinese men lay motionless in pools of blood, unconscious, critically wounded, facing death.

People from many countries, especially Asia, have sought work in Israel because of its booming economy. Their goal has been to earn enough money for their own needs with some left over to send back to their families.

This had probably been the reason those two Chinese men were in Israel—men who now lay dying in the street, victims of someone else's war.

The deafening shrill of sirens pierced the air as two ambulances arrived with emergency lights flashing. Medical personnel quickly began the triage of mangled bodies. Some of the injured stood stunned, bloody, and silent. Others sat in disbelief as they surveyed their wounded bodies. The two Chinese men were the most critically wounded, so they were quickly placed on stretchers and loaded into the first ambulance. With sirens wailing, the victims were rushed to the emergency room of Shaare'i Zedek, the hospital where I was on duty as a medical student.

From Russia to Israel

Tanya Kovtun was indeed a long way from home. Born in far eastern Russia, she had taken advantage of a rare opportunity to study in Alaska her last year of high school. Financial support from Christian friends enabled her to stay in Alaska on a student visa to attend university. Even though she graduated with honors from the University of Alaska, her desire to go to medical school seemed an impossible dream. Her prayers were answered when a letter of acceptance finally came from Columbia University School of Medicine. But her acceptance was not for study in New York; it was for their new program of International Health and Medicine in Israel.

Tanya arrived in Jerusalem to begin her medical school training at the time of some of the bloodiest fighting in Israel. She had grown up in a Communist country, had become a Christian while studying in America, and was now positioned in the middle of a terrible war between Israeli Jews and Palestinian Muslims.

On the Friday morning of the bombing, Tanya had to quickly step aside to avoid being hit by the emergency room cart as it whizzed by. Knowing it carried her patient to examine and follow, she made her way to the examination cubicle and parted the curtains. What she saw will never be erased from her memory.

> I saw the nurses turning the patient on his side—but, actually, I didn't think of the "thing" I was seeing as a human being. It was just a torso, missing all four limbs and with the face so swollen that it didn't bear any resemblance to a human face. The body, or what was left of it, looked like a swollen balloon with some black hair on top.
>
> I entered the cubicle and took my turn examining the patient, finding that he was in a coma but his pulse, blood pressure, and breathing were normal. The doctors around me were looking at the patient's chart and talking about the victim's electrolyte disturbances and his temperature, but my mind was in shock, and I found myself unable to pay attention to what I heard being discussed.
>
> I was so shaken up by the tragedy of the situation that nothing else seemed to matter. As the first shock wave passed I was ashamed of myself. How dare I think of this human being as a "thing"? Seeing him as something dead? He was still breathing and his heart was beating, so my responsibility was to do everything possible to keep him alive!
>
> But the reality stayed the same: even if this man survived, he would be an invalid for the rest of his life. He wouldn't be able to work and support his family anymore.

He would have to be taken back to China where he would be dependent upon his relatives for care, and eventually he would probably die of poverty and disease.

I thought, *What evil in this world is so great that an innocent man from China can suffer injuries so devastating at the hands of a terrorist from Palestine that his body is literally torn apart in this way? How is it that the responsibility for his care in this tragic moment falls into the hands of doctors and nurses of the Jewish faith in Jerusalem, so far from his home? What a strange situation for a young Russian Christian girl like me to have the honor and the challenge of joining in the urgent effort to save the life of this Chinese man whose innocent blood covers my hands and stains my white coat!*

The patient died the following day without us ever even knowing his name. Many thoughts and questions flooded my mind: *Did he know the Lord? Was he miserable and lonely on that fateful Friday morning, the beginning of the last day of his life? What will his family do now? Will his name ever be known so that his family can be notified of his tragic death at the hands of a terrorist?*

My heart was so heavy I went back to my dorm and cried. I cried for this man's purposeless death and for hundreds of other equally purposeless deaths that happened in other terrorist attacks in Israel and other places in the world. I cried for the Holy Land that is torn apart by war and hatred. I cried for eighteen-year-old boys who walk around with semiautomatic weapons. I thought how foolish people are. How God has provided everything for us to live peacefully and happily, and yet we choose to live in turmoil and hatred and with the terrible sadness that follows. So I prayed for Palestinian people and Israeli people, since both are suffering greatly.

I don't remember everything I prayed about then, but I felt the burden lifted from my heart. At that moment I really understood what it is like to see a light in the darkness. Jesus is our light. In the midst of this dangerous, hateful, insane, and greedy world, Jesus Christ is the light that leads us to peace, purpose, and sanity. I have never felt that more clearly than on that day. And another thing I will never forget will be the instant I first saw the mutilated body of that Chinese man who was an innocent victim of the hatred that exists between people. People created by God who are of different faiths and cannot find a peaceful way to live together in one country.

Thwarted Plans

Tanya Kovtun's early years were blessed by growing up in a happy home. She never minded living in an isolated town, perched right on the edge of the Bering Strait. When she came to America and developed friendships with Christians in her teens, she readily identified with the love of Jesus Christ and accepted Him as Lord and Savior.

My association with Tanya began with a telephone call from Franklin Graham in August 1995. He asked if I would go to Provideniya, a remote former military outpost in far eastern Russia. Franklin told me about the Christian ministry that Glenn Alsworth, owner of a flying service in Alaska, was developing in Provideniya and of the healthcare needs of the people there.

From Anchorage Airport a small Cessna aircraft took me to Lake Clark, an hour's flying time west of Anchorage. The next morning I was to fly to Nome to refuel the aircraft for the two-hour flight across the Bering Strait to Provideniya. However, we awoke to a heavy fog that grounded our non-instrument-rated aircraft. The next four days gave me an opportunity to talk with Dan Waggoner, the young pastor at Lake Clark. In 1992 he flew to Provideniya with Glenn Alsworth to hold the first of many Bible study meetings with young people in that remote Soviet outpost. Later he brought small groups of these young students back to Alaska to stay as guests in Glenn and Patty's home so they could attend school at Port Alsworth. Seventeen-year-old Tanya Kovtun, part of the group flown to Lake Clark in August 1995, had been at Port Alsworth only a few days when I arrived to await flying on to Provideniya. On Sunday morning, as I sat waiting for the skies to clear, Dan Waggoner asked me to speak during the church service. About forty of the Port Alsworth staff assembled in the meeting room that morning, and one of them was Tanya.

After five days, I could wait no longer for the weather to clear enough for me to fly on to Russia, so I returned to California and my neurosurgical practice. In October I returned to Anchorage, this time with Sylvia, a team of two dentists, and a dental assistant. Our mission was to try again to fly to Provideniya. Dick Page met us with the Piper Navajo and a young Russian girl who would act as our interpreter—Tanya Kovtun.

We took off for Nome, knowing the already short days in Alaska meant most of our flight would be in darkness. After refueling at Nome Airport, we headed across the Bering Strait for Russia. As we neared Russian air space, Dick Page tried to make radio contact with the control tower in Provideniya, but Russian air-traffic control refused to respond. Dick knew entering Russian air space in the darkness and without permission from Soviet air-traffic control was not possible. Our only option was to return to Nome.

Flying over the wide expanse of open seas in the blackness of that night enabled us to witness a brilliant display of the aurora borealis, and we marveled at this beautiful miracle of God's magnificent creation. After landing safely and securing the aircraft, we got some sleep in preparation for trying again to reach Russia.

During the night several inches of snow and ice covered our plane. It was bitterly cold as we began clearing the wings and fuselage of the aircraft using our plastic ID badges and credit cards. Tanya Kovtun recorded in her journal the events of that very cold, body-numbing October morning at Nome Airport.

> My student ID sure came in handy! It was twenty degrees below zero in Nome, Alaska, and I was using my ID to scrape ice off the window of a Navajo (an eight-passenger airplane). My hands were freezing, my nose was bright red, and my teeth were chattering, but all I could think about was that scraping right next to me was a world-renowned neurosurgeon. (I was also wishing for some hot coffee, but that was secondary.) We were preparing to fly across the Bering Strait to Provideniya, Russia, for a mission trip arranged by the organization Samaritan's Purse. I was to go as a translator for a group of doctors, one of whom was Dr. Cheatham. I was especially excited to work with him since it was he who inspired me first to dream of and then to actually pursue a career as a doctor.
>
> I had first come to Alaska with the intention of studying languages. When I heard Dr. Cheatham speak of his own experiences as a doctor, though, it seemed as if everything about my life fell into place. It became very clear that being a doctor was something I wanted to do for the rest of my life. He spoke of being in Bosnia and how it didn't matter

what side the soldier was from; if he needed medical care he received it. That impressed me. It seemed as though being a doctor superseded all the war and the hate that surrounds us. I wanted to be part of that! Little did I know that three months later I would be on a mission trip assisting Dr. Cheatham and two dentists as an interpreter.

I had already been exposed to the medical profession because my mom is a surgical nurse. I always admired the field, yet I never considered it for myself. Translating for the doctors gave me the opportunity to make it personal. I learned two main things on this trip. First, I realized how important communication between the patient and the doctor is. Most of my time was spent assisting dental teams. Dancing back and forth across the language barrier was very challenging. Those people depended on me to tell the doctor exactly what was bothering them, and to accurately describe to them the treatment that was going to be used. I also found out how important it was for the patients to hear a comforting word or two, as they lay there on the dental chair ready for the worst. Second was seeing the doctors' concern for their patients as being more important than their own comfort. This was evidenced by their willingness to work in the most remote and forgotten regions where the lack of medical help was apparent. I saw how very important and needed medical professionals were. My slowly growing dream of becoming a doctor was beginning to cry for action.

When the mission trip was over and I returned to my studies at the University of Alaska, I began taking premed requirements and declared a biology major. Whenever I found myself struggling with a class or doubting my resolve, something encouraging seemed to happen. I was able to spend a few days volunteering in the Radiology Department of Providence Alaska Medical Center. I was also able to translate for two other medical teams who were visiting Provideniya.

Dr. Cheatham has inspired me to strive not only to be a doctor but an excellent one. I don't want to be mediocre in what I do, or ever to "just get by." I want to be a doctor whom people can put their trust in, someone they know they can talk to and ask questions of. I never want to forget what it feels like to be struggling to achieve a dream that sometimes seems impossible. By remembering how I feel right now, I'll be better able to encourage and inspire future students who dream as I do. I hope to set a high standard and example in front of them so that they never lose sight of what a great profession we pursue. That standard and example has been set in front of me, and it is what I am most thankful for.

We finally took off from Nome, flew across the Bering Strait without incident, and landed on the airstrip at Provideniya, Russia, a small, desolate town. During the Cold War, an estimated two-hundred and fifty thousand Russian troops were positioned there, ready to respond in case of attack by U.S. forces. Now the population of Provideniya is progressively declining due to lack of jobs and a failing economy. Its buildings and infrastructure are in decay.

With Tanya Kovtun acting as an interpreter our Samaritan's Purse team set up basic dental clinics and were able to begin the process of providing medical equipment and supplies for Provideniya Hospital.

After that trip, Tanya returned to her studies at the University of Alaska to pursue her dream that took her to Israel where she came face to face with the man from China who had become the latest victim of a female Palestinian terrorist bomber.

What a contrast can be seen between the lives of these two young women. One a terrorist who hated others enough to blow herself up in order to kill them, knowing that as a female she would not even qualify for the believed "entrance into paradise" that supposedly awaits male Islamic suicide terrorists. The other young woman was Tanya Kovtun, a young lady with so much love in her heart that her life's goal is to give help to as many people as possible during their time of greatest need. The reward she seeks is to live her life in a way pleasing and acceptable to a loving God.

The lives of these two young women define the battle under way in our dangerous world today—the battle between hatred and violence on one hand, and love and compassion on the other. This battle has become totally relevant to all people as we find ourselves living with the reality of international terrorism. Even in America, we have seen the evils of terrorism come to our own shores. During World War I, a popular song was entitled, "Over There, Over There." Its lyrics identified the fact that for Americans, the war was "over there" and not here. But this war of our time is "over here," at home where we live, and we must deal with the question of what we are going to do about it.

On May 27, 2003, Tanya Kovtun received her Doctor of Medicine degree from Columbia University. With God's leading and with His blessing she has achieved the impossible. Now Tanya is in a residency program, training to become a general surgeon as further preparation for doing medical mission work she feels called to do. Her story powerfully confirms the fact that a person can step forward from humble beginnings, say, "Yes, Lord, I'll go; send me," and be used by the Lord in a mighty way to make a difference. With God's help, all things are possible.

We have been called to be servants of others. A servant is one who *gives*. The way in which each one of us is able to be of service to others in their time of need varies according to our individual talents, resources, ages, locations, the state of our health, and the responsibilities we carry. But Jesus said that even giving a cup of cool water to a person who is thirsty is like giving the cup to Him. The important thing is not what we are *able* to give, but that we *do* give to others in need.

Shoeboxes and Sheets

Jim Hodges is someone who lives to give. He is a successful businessman whose company makes cardboard boxes. From one of his warehouses Jim also carries out a supplemental feeding program, supplying sacks of groceries and other household essentials to needy people through churches.

Jim has traveled with Samaritan's Purse teams to Bosnia, Mexico, Kosovo, several countries in Africa, India, and even North Korea. Several years ago, while Jim was on a trip around the world with Sylvia and me, I had an opportunity to introduce him to Franklin Graham. We had just flown into Nairobi from Uganda; Franklin had just flown in from North Africa.

As Franklin, Jim, and I stood talking at the Samaritan's Purse Guest House in Nairobi, the conversation turned to the Operation Christmas Child program. Jim said, "It concerns me that some people may not fill a shoebox with gifts for children because they don't have an empty shoebox to use. I make boxes in my business. So what if I make some boxes that are just like shoeboxes for you to give to people and ask them to fill them with gifts for children?"

Franklin responded, "You mean you could make some boxes for us?"

"Yes," Jim said. "I can make them just the way you want them and print whatever you want on them—in six colors! And I will ship them to churches wherever you want."

I could hear the excitement in Franklin's voice when he said, "Jim, that sounds like a good idea! It would give pastors an opportunity to provide people with an empty box to fill with things for a little child. Then the church could have a time of dedication when all of the filled boxes could be brought back and prayed over in a worship service. How many of these boxes could you make for us? A thousand?"

Jim Hodges didn't hesitate a second before saying, "How about starting with one hundred thousand and then see how it goes from there? And remember, this is something I want to do at no cost to Samaritan's Purse."

Since first meeting with Franklin, Jim has manufactured nearly five million shoeboxes for Operation Christmas Child, making it possible for this many additional children to receive gifts. These brightly colored green and red boxes have the Operation Christmas Child logo printed on them, and they have been the encouragement necessary for many, many people to become involved in this wonderful ministry. Jim Hodges took the thing he knew best—making boxes—and turned it into a ministry in support of the work of Samaritan's Purse, to make a difference by reaching out to children around the world. But supplying empty shoeboxes for the Operation Christmas Child program at Samaritan's Purse was not enough for Jim Hodges. He is also using one of his warehouses to collect medical equipment and supplies that he can ship to Samaritan's Purse and other Christian ministries.

Franklin has also built a medical equipment warehouse at

Samaritan's Purse in Boone, North Carolina, where he receives surplus and refurbished medical equipment and supplies for Christian mission hospitals and projects around the world.

There may not be any place in the world that is more dangerous than the Congo in Central African Republic. There are estimates that as many as three million people have been killed in that country in recent years, and stories of brutal torture, murder, and even cannibalism are common in today's news. Sylvia and I have made a number of short-term medical mission trips to Nyankunde Mission Hospital in the Congo, located near the town of Bunia. The needs in that remote hospital were so great that patients often had to lie on rubber-matted hospital beds without sheets.

When the tribal wars in the Congo were beginning several years ago, we agreed to make another visit to Nyankunde and to take a critically needed gastroscope with us. Because of the high rate of stomach diseases among the people in that part of the Congo, missionary doctors had asked Samaritan's Purse to provide a gastroscope, a long, tubelike fiberoptic instrument that is passed through the mouth into the esophagus and stomach. New gastroscopes cost about ten thousand dollars each, but the Lord provided one through Samaritan's Purse for use at Nyankunde. And just before we left for Africa two committed Christian friends, Roger and Carmen Shea, made enough brand-new bedsheets available to fill six duffel bags for us to take with us. Inside one of the duffel bags we hid the gastroscope between layers of sheets, praying it would not be stolen en route.

When we landed at the small Bunia airport, the political and military situation was tense. I was taken, along with the six duffel bags, into a hot and humid room in which eight mean-looking Congolese officials stood waiting. They ordered me to sit down.

While the others stood surrounding me, the chief government official questioned me concerning my purpose in coming to the Congo. He also wanted to know what was inside the duffel bags. I told him I didn't have keys to open them, which was true because Sylvia had them in her backpack. He remained suspicious concerning the reason for our team's visit.

For forty-five minutes the grilling continued, and I kept wiping perspiration from my face. It was very intimidating, sitting there surrounded by men towering over me. And each time I tried to stand up, they told me to "sit down." Finally, the chief government official said I could continue our flight to Nyankunde, but he was impounding the six bags "for further inspection." I protested explaining how embarrassing it would be to arrive at Nyankunde Hospital without the bags, so the official said, "You may take one of the bags with you."

Our team reboarded the small missionary airplane, and one duffel bag was loaded onboard with us. We took off from the landing strip as quickly as possible. Upon arrival at Nyankunde I quickly opened the bag and found the gastroscope hidden inside between layers of protective sheets! We thanked God for having provided safe passage for this item of medical equipment, so critically needed to help treat patients at Nyankunde Hospital. The following day the other five duffel bags were released by the government official who said, "You may have these. They are filled only with sheets and are of no use to us."

But what about you? What do you feel God is calling you to do to make a difference, and while doing so share with others the story of Jesus? Whatever it is that God is calling you to give to others in His name, you can be sure that He will bless your work if it brings help to others and brings honor to Him.

Before you turn the page, ask yourself these questions:

- How strong is my commitment to give of myself in order to help others?
- Have I asked God through prayer how and what He wants me to give?
- Am I prepared to share the fullness of a Christian life with others?

chapter 6

God Will Bless What We Give

For I was hungry and you gave Me food; I was thirsty and you gave Me drink; I was a stranger and you took Me in; I was naked and you clothed Me; I was sick and you visited Me; I was in prison and you came to Me.

—MATTHEW 25:35–40

I have two kidneys, and I will give one of them to you so that you can live."

IMAGINE what these eighteen words would mean to you, if you were experiencing kidney failure, were being kept alive with daily dialysis treatments, and knew your only real hope lay in receiving a donor kidney. Then imagine your doctors had already told you that because of your age you were not eligible for having your name placed on the already inadequate list for available donor kidneys. What if Bernie and Marianne Morton, a couple who lived in the same area as you, but whom you didn't really know that well, came to your home to inquire about how you were getting along? And imagine that as you told them the bad news you had received from your doctors, you heard Marianne Morton say, "I'll give you one of my kidneys."

Neighbors do give things to each other sometimes: a cup of sugar, some grass seed for a bad spot in the lawn, or the loan of a garden tool. But for a neighbor to give a kidney, without a moment's hesitation and to a neighbor she didn't really know very well?

The kidney patient and his wife were so astounded they began to cry for joy. But Marianne Morton, a deeply committed Christian, was only responding to the command of Jesus to "love your neighbor as you love yourself." Marianne's blood sample proved to be a match for the man. Then she followed through with her offer to risk her own life in order to *give* one of her kidneys to that person whose life depended upon his receiving it. She did this because of God's love for her, and because she so deeply believes Jesus's command to love others applies directly to her. Today, her neighbor is enjoying good health, and he feels eternally grateful for the "love in action" shown to him by Marianne Morton in his time of need.

Marianne and Bernie chuckle at the symbolism of the gift she gave, since she is a Christian, and the man to whom she gave one of her kidneys is a Jew. She was born and raised in Germany, the country where during World War II the Nazis killed several Jewish family members of the man who received her kidney. Marianne says of this, "I can't undo the Holocaust, but giving this man one of my kidneys in his time of need is a way that I, as a German, can give something back to a Jewish person."

During a quiet moment of reflection, ask yourself if *you* would be willing to say to a neighbor in need, "I have two kidneys, and I will give one of them to you so that you can live." And if so, would you still have enough love in your heart to do this if you were an immigrant to the U.S. from Germany and your neighbor in need of a kidney was a person of another faith, or no faith at all? And what if that "neighbor" wasn't someone you knew very well who just happened to live in your town or city?

Marianne now says of the gift she made:

> This whole matter is not really much of a story. Someone needed something that I could give, and the most rewarding aspect for me has been that now I get to see the kidney at work each day, in a person living nearby whose life depended upon receiving it. Most of all, I am just trying to be obedient to the Lord and striving to be a good example of His love. I believe this incident has shown my neighbor what it means to be a Christian. As my husband Bernie has said with a thoughtful smile, "A German Christian kidney at work in a Jewish body; who knows where it will lead! If each one of us who is a Christian can bring just one other person into a loving, personal relationship with Jesus, what a wonderful world this will be."

Most people in the world don't understand the depth of God's love and don't obey His greatest commandment to love Him totally and completely. Neither do they obey His commandment to love our neighbor as we love ourselves. Marianne's love for her neighbor is probably confusing to many people. An offer like this carries risk of loss of one's life, guaranteed physical pain, and a long surgical scar to be worn by the donor as a permanent reminder. For Marianne Morton, giving one of her kidneys meant going through extensive physical examinations, blood tests, CT scans, ultrasounds, and other means of evaluation to make sure she was healthy and that her kidney would be a match. Their operations were scheduled at the same time, and Marianne's took the longest.

Her first words on awakening from the anesthetic were, "How is my neighbor doing?"

A Man Who Loved His Neighbor

I personally experienced the kind of genuine, God-inspired, unconditional love that Marianne Morton showed to her neighbor. The person who made a choice to give his life in order that I might live was a humble Bosnian neurosurgeon named Dr. Josip Jurisic. It was a bitterly cold, cloudy, rainy afternoon as Sylvia and I and seven other members of a Samaritan's Purse neurosurgical team landed in Sarajevo onboard a United Nations cargo plane. It was October 1993, and our team had come there to operate on people who were casualties in a bitter war of ethnic cleansing.

In military helmets and twenty-five-pound flak jackets, we quickly crossed the runway to find shelter behind highly stacked sandbags and steel barriers under what had been Sarajevo's airport terminal. We waited until the darkness to be transported in an armored personnel carrier to a place where we spent the night with six hundred UN soldiers. In the villages of the surrounding countryside, people huddled in the basements of their shelled and burned homes, with no heat, no water, and little food.

The following morning when we first entered the hospital in which we were to work, we passed stacks of machine guns and automatic rifles that had been checked at the door. The building was cold. The light was dim. The air was heavy. The scene was awful! As we passed from ward to ward in that large hospital, we saw rows upon rows of beds in which lay the broken, bandaged bodies of men and women scarred by war. Some were paralyzed. Some were in coma. Many were missing arms and legs. Most of them just stared in silence, as if they had no hope. These were people, just like you and me, who had been beaten up by neighbors filled with ethnic hatred while most of the world simply walked on by, ignoring the war because they didn't want to get involved.

As a physician, I knew that many of these injured patients were going to die unless someone cared enough to help. That's when I met him, a man with love and compassion in his heart. Dr. Josip Jurisic had the thin, gaunt face of a man who had lost sixty-two pounds in eighteen months because he didn't have enough to eat. Though he was just thirty-nine years old, he looked sixty. He led me through the hospital he called home. His English was a little broken but his courage was crystal-clear. This man was the only neurosurgeon in a six-hundred-bed hospital, in the middle of a war. This was headquarters hospital for the Bosnian Muslim Army and was filled to overflowing with fifteen hundred patients, nearly every one a casualty of war.

Imagine one of these patients was someone *you* loved—your husband, your wife, your child or best friend—and needed surgery to remove fragments of bullet or bone from his/her brain, or pieces of shrapnel from his/her spine. Imagine knowing that if the operation wasn't done soon, your loved one would almost certainly die. Then imagine meeting the one doctor who was able to perform the necessary surgery in the midst of exploding mortar shells and cannon fire, in the sights of a sniper's rifle, and under the confines of frequent power failure even from the hospital's emergency generator. That's what it was like for me when I met Dr. Josip, a modern-day good Samaritan.

Every day in that cavernous hospital, I walked beside Dr. Josip, and watched him care for strangers who had been beaten, wounded, abandoned, and forgotten. It was clear to me that he was a man who had incredible love and compassion in his heart and that he was totally committed to using his abilities in bringing help to others. What was it, I wondered, about Dr. Josip that allowed him to so freely give himself to others? What made him want to help the needy along the side of life's road when so many others would simply choose to walk on by? How did this good Samaritan find a way to love when so many others, perhaps like you and me, simply want to find an excuse for not getting involved? As Dr. Josip and I worked together each day, I often wondered if I would have the commitment and the courage to do what he was doing. I knew that in a few days, I'd leave Bosnia and return to my home and that he would still be there, in the middle of a war, working to save lives.

How can he keep giving day after day? I wondered. Then, a few days later, Dr. Josip amazed me with the answer. He reached in his wallet, took out a crinkled-up photograph and said to me, "This is me saying good-bye to my wife and small son as they were being evacuated from Sarajevo at the beginning of the war." The photo showed Dr. Josip standing alongside the bus. His hand was on the outside of the bus window pressed against the outstretched hand of his young son on the inside of the bus, who in that moment wanted just one more time to touch his daddy. At that moment they were separated only by the thickness of a pane of glass, but it was a separation Dr. Josip realized might be for the rest of their lives.

"My pregnant wife waved and my son waved and I waved," he said. "And that was it. The bus left. I watched until there was nothing left but a few whiffs of diesel exhaust, and they were gone. Then I went back inside the hospital and began caring for yet another patient, then another, then another."

Dr. Josip told me how after seeing his family safely sent away, he prayed God might protect his wife, small son, and unborn baby, and then he said, "My life is in Your hands. Please use me to care for the people who are being wounded in this terrible war."

I believe that as he looked into the eyes of his hurting patients, he saw the tears of his own wife and small son, and that prepared him to give his own life, if necessary, in order to bring help and hope to others. Out of his own pain, Dr. Josip found a new compassion, a new way of showing love and compassion that says to another, "I know what you're feeling. I know what it's like to hurt. By sharing what I have with you, God will turn my heartache into your blessing."

His Life for Mine

One afternoon I found out just how much Dr. Josip was willing to give to another when he assisted me as I operated on a soldier of the Bosnian Muslim Army. The soldier had been shot through the neck and was paralyzed from the neck down. In removing the bullet that had shattered his spine, I found it had blown his spinal cord in two and knew he would remain paralyzed for the rest of his life. The soldier had not been breathing very well when he arrived at the hospital. Knowing that because of paralysis of his chest muscles he would continue to have difficulty breathing after the surgery, we left the tube in his airway, placing him on a ventilator to help him breathe. The ventilator was powered with an electrical generator using diesel fuel because the hospital had electric power only intermittently.

The next morning as we made our rounds, Dr. Josip took me aside to a quiet corner where it was safe to talk and told me the bad news about the paralyzed soldier. "During the night the supply of diesel fuel ran out, the generator quit working, his ventilator stopped, and he could not breathe on his own, so he died."

Naturally I was sad, but what Dr. Josip said next to me stunned me and caused me to tremble all over. "Professor," he said, "because it was you who operated on the soldier and he died, I fear his people will come for you and will kill you. Therefore, I have changed the medical record. I have erased your name as the surgeon, and I have written my name in place of yours."

For a long moment I looked into the eyes of this compassionate man. My throat became dry and I could feel a large lump forming that I couldn't swallow away. Finally I said to Dr. Josip, "But surely, my friend, that means they will come for you and will kill you."

Dr. Josip said quietly, "You can leave this place of war, and I cannot. I am prepared to die in your place, if I must, in order that you might live."

In that moment, years of Sunday school, sermons, and books about the Christian life fell away. When I looked at this caring physician, holding the operative report with his name in place of mine, I thought of the Great Physician, Jesus Christ, who was willing to take my place and die for me on the cross.

Dr. Josip's story holds the key to why you and I are called to *love* and to *give*. It is because as John 3:16 says, "God so loved the world, that He gave His only Son . . ." to die on the cross at Calvary in order that those who believe in Him can experience God's gift of being able to live with Him in heaven throughout eternity.

God protected us from harm. Soldiers did not return to kill me or Dr. Josip, whose life was spared because they needed him alive, to operate on the war wounded. He continued to live and work in dangerous surroundings long after we left Sarajevo and returned to the United States.

In spite of the very dangerous situations in which he found himself, Dr. Josip remained focused upon doing what he felt God had called him to do, and that was to provide loving, compassionate care to victims of the terrible war that had come to his beloved homeland. Later in the war in Bosnia I was able see him there and to operate with him again. After the fighting stopped, he was named chief of neurosurgery at Sarajevo's State Hospital. His wife gave birth to a little girl soon after they were evacuated from Sarajevo, and Dr. Josip's son is now in medical school.

On two occasions Dr. Josip has come to the U.S. and shared his testimony at the Samaritan's Purse Prescription for Hope Conference at the Billy Graham Training Center. On his first visit there he accepted Jesus Christ as his Lord and Savior, an opportunity not previously extended to him in his native Bosnia. Dr. Josip has been a guest in our home, and it always warms my heart to have him telephone me from Sarajevo and say, "Hello, Professor. It is Josip here," and then add, "you are my 'brover.'"

VERY EARLY on the morning of September 12, 2001, I was awakened by a telephone call with these words: "Hello, Professor. It is Josip, in Sarajevo. My heart is broken as I have heard of the terrible suicide bombing of your buildings in New York and Washington and the tragic loss of innocent lives. I need to know that you and Sylvia and your family are safe from harm."

I told Dr. Josip that we were well and how much I appreciated his call and his words of great concern for our country and for the American people. Then he said, "Please tell Dr. Billy Graham and Reverend Franklin that Josip will come! I will come to New York and help operate on the wounded people if I am needed. I will never forget how you and the Samaritan's Purse team came to my country during the darkest days of war in Bosnia and how you operated on the wounded. And now it will be my privilege to come to America during this darkest hour for you. If I am needed, I will come."

Dr. Josip Jurisic is truly my brother. On September 12, 2001, the tables were turned, and he was ready to give of himself and his abilities in order to help people in America who had been wounded in the terrorist attack on the preceding day.

"God so loved the world that He gave . . ." The Bible tells us that God gave to us, and that we are to give from our abundance to others. If we are to learn to give, we first need to remember how abundantly God has given to us.

A Powerful Dream

Marilyn Henderson Smythe was making a trip around the world with Sylvia and me, visiting Christian mission hospitals and Samaritan's Purse projects. We were in Kenya, spending the night at a game lodge. Sylvia and I were awakened early by the roar of lions nearby. After getting dressed we walked to the game lodge for some hot coffee and breakfast and found Marilyn was already there.

"Mel," she said, "I had a dream last night, and I would like to tell you and the rest of our group about it during our time of devotions this morning."

I explained to Marilyn that one of the other team members had already prepared to give the morning devotions but that she could tell us about her dream that evening after dinner. As we continued our journey toward Tenwek Hospital that day, Marilyn asked me again if she could tell about her dream. I could tell it had powerfully impacted her and that she was anxious to share it as soon as possible. Still, I encouraged her to wait until after dinner that evening so that she would have the undivided attention of the team.

Finally the time had come. After finishing dinner I said, "OK, Marilyn, tell us about your dream."

Marilyn began,

> Well, this dream last night was so real and vivid that I couldn't get back to sleep. I just sat there in my room, listening to the lions roaring and waiting for the sunrise.
>
> In the dream I was sitting at my desk with a large book before me. Then in my dream I heard God's voice speaking to me, saying, "Marilyn, open the book."
>
> As I opened the book and started turning the pages, I found that many of the pages were blank. On some of the pages there was printing, and as I read I found they described how on that day I had prayed to God asking Him for His help in some way. Reading on I could see that on every occasion He had answered my prayer, giving me some wonderful blessing in response to my having asked Him for help. In my dream as I looked at the pages with writing on them, I excitedly said to God, "I remember that day! I remember it was a very happy time in my life because I prayed for Your help during a time of need, and You answered my prayer and blessed me." Even though I noticed His blessing had not always been what I had wanted to hear, it had proven to be the right answer for dealing with the need I had prayed for. But, as I turned page after page in the book, I began to noticed that many of the pages were blank, and I asked God why.
>
> Then God said to me, "Marilyn, the book before you is the book of your life. Each page in your book that has something written on it means that on that day you prayed to me, asking Me for something. As you have noticed, on those days that you prayed to Me, I always answered your prayer and met your need with a wonderful gift as a special

blessing for you. And you accepted it as a gift from Me and remembered to thank Me for it." Then God continued, "But notice how many blank pages there are in your life book. These pages represent the days when you either didn't call upon My name for help, or you didn't remember to thank Me for the gift I blessed you with."

I could feel a big lump forming in my throat and tears welling up in my eyes as I said, "Father, why didn't You go ahead and give me gifts and blessings on every day of my life?"

God's voice said, "Marilyn, I *did* give you great gifts and wonderful blessings on each and every day of your life. But it wasn't very often that you asked Me for that blessing or gift, and even less often that you took time to thank Me for the gifts and blessings I had given to you."

Through sobbing tears I said to God in my dream, "Why? Why have You cared enough to love me and bless me every day of my life when I haven't taken time to speak to You in prayer about a need or to give thanks to You."

Then I could feel this wonderful blanket of love enveloping me as I heard the Lord speaking to me softly, "What I have done for you, I have done because I love you. Go now and give to others from the abundance I have blessed you with, sharing My love with them."

By this time tears were streaming down Marilyn's cheeks. "I have been so anxious all day to tell each of you about my dream. It was so real, and it so deeply touched my heart that I wanted to share it with you. Each day for the rest of my life I plan to stop and lift my eyes toward heaven and open my heart to my loving heavenly Father. I plan to take time to ask Him for His help each day and then to remember to thank Him for the many blessings He bestows upon me. I want each and every single page in my book of life to be filled with the words He has written upon it."

It took a brutal war to bring Dr. Josip Jurisic close enough to the Lord that he could hear God's voice speaking to him. He had to be brought to his knees with sadness and grief before he could know the importance of praying to God, asking Him for His special blessing and the importance of giving thanks to Him. For Marilyn Henderson Smythe, it was seeing the needs of suffering people in Kenya that prepared her heart and mind to hear God speak to her through a very vivid dream so real that her life has been forever changed.

SURPRISE!

The reason God has called you and me to *love* and to *give* came to me many times and in powerful ways while Sylvia and I were in Bosnia in 1993 operating on the war wounded. On one particular occasion, soldiers from the British battalion of the United Nations provided a military escort for our Samaritan's Purse team as we crossed enemy lines to work at a place called Nova Bila. This was a village in a valley where eighteen thousand Croatian people lived, surrounded by Bosnian Muslim Army forces. In the basement of the church at Nova Bila, I performed brain surgery on a young man who had been shot in the head by enemy forces. Dr. Bruno Buzuk, the village dentist interpreted for me as I taught the general surgeon at Nova Bila church-hospital how to operate on patients with bullets in their brains.

Dr. Bruno was a very friendly young man, and his wife showed her love and appreciation for our team's visit by preparing warm bean soup and baked bread for us to eat. I came to admire Bruno, a dentist who had been required to apply his dental skills and act as a medical doctor to help care for the war wounded. I was extremely impressed by the compassionate work I saw him do, and felt grateful for the help he gave interpreting as I operated with doctors who spoke another language.

After we returned to the U.S., word came through a Canadian relief worker that Bruno had been killed by snipers. I felt very sad and felt a great sense of loss in hearing this terrible news.

Two years after the war ended, Sylvia and I returned to Nova Bila, this time leading a Samaritan's Purse Operation Christmas Child team. When our vehicle entered the Nova Bila village square we could not have been more surprised! The village leaders had set up a stage complete with public address system, and the local band was playing our national anthem to greet us. It appeared that all of the people in the village had come to the square to welcome us.

We were led up the steps to the stage where the mayor offered words of welcome, and a beautiful little girl in national costume presented Sylvia with a large bouquet of red roses. A choir of children sang songs for us, and the village band played. I was asked to speak and extended greetings from Franklin Graham and Samaritan's Purse. Then our team handed out shoebox gifts to all of the children. It was a never-to-be-forgotten occasion with the people seeming to say thank you, because our Samaritan's Purse neurosurgical team had come to Nova Bila during their darkest hour.

After the ceremony in the village square, our team was taken to the parish church at Nova Bila, where several doctors we had worked with two years before greeted us. As we sat in the church rectory having coffee and, trying to communicate with each other I said, "I was so sad to hear that Bruno had been killed. I wish he could have lived to be here with us today."

The doctor who could speak some English spoke to the others for a moment, as if searching for the words to say. Then he turned back to me, smiled happily, and in broken English said, "Bruno lives! He is coming back!" At that moment the door to the rectory swung open and in walked Bruno! Believing Bruno to be dead and suddenly seeing him alive and coming back to receive us, with outstretched, open arms and with a smile on his face, was an awesome experience!

Bruno shook hands with Sylvia and me, gave each of us a big hug, and began telling us how good it was to see us again. Then he related that, a short time after we left Nova Bila, he was on his way home from the hospital when snipers started shooting at him. Driving at a high speed in an effort to escape, he lost control of his car, crashed into a building, and was rendered unconscious. People brought Bruno to Nova Bila church-hospital, where he remained in a deep coma for over a month and nearly died. The first thing he remembered after the accident was awakening to see a woman he did not know standing at the side of his bed and holding a wedding photograph in front of him, saying, "Bruno, I am your wife. This is our wedding picture."

Bruno was completely paralyzed on his right side, had difficulty speaking, and was unable to recognize his wife, children, friends, and fellow workers for several more weeks. Then his memory slowly began to return, but the paralysis of his right arm and leg remained. He was evacuated to a hospital in Split, on the Adriatic Coast, and later was flown to a rehabilitation hospital in Germany.

Bruno recalls this experience:

> I felt very depressed, being paralyzed on my right side and believing I would never walk again or be able to perform dentistry. I prayed to God that He would give healing to

> my body. I tried very hard to make things better. Then one day, I looked at my right index finger and saw it move slightly. A sudden thrill of excitement passed through my body because now I had hope.
>
> For three months I worked very hard with the therapist, and little by little movement came back in my right arm and leg, and my thinking and memory returned, at least all but the one month I lay in a coma. Now I am able to practice as a dentist again, and I give thanks to God for this.

God so *loved* Bruno that He *gave to* him His blessing by restoring his paralyzed body to health. We thought Bruno had died, but through God's grace we were able to see that Bruno lives. How symbolic of God's love for us and the truth that, although He died on the cross for the forgiveness of our sins, Jesus lives and one day He is coming back, to greet us with open arms, taking us with Him to receive God's gift of life eternal.

Has anything happened in your life to cause you to be still, and listen, in order that you might hear what God is saying to you?

When you do hear God's voice speaking to you, the Bible says He will be telling you to *love* Him totally, completely, and without exception, and He wants you to show His love to others. Also, He wants you to *give* of yourself and your resources to your neighbors as an expression of His love.

Marianne Morton, Josip Jurisic, Marilyn Symthe, and Bruno Buzuk are all faithfully serving the Lord, each doing their work right at home where they live—each one experiencing the joy of loving and serving, doing so in God's name and for His glory.

But what about you? Have you found that one thing God wants you to do in serving Him?

Before you turn the page, ask yourself these questions:

- What am I prepared to give to help another? My love? My kidney? My life?
- Am I able to hear God's voice as He speaks to me?
- Am I ready for that unique and special way God has in mind for me to give?

PART 3

The Trust to Believe

chapter 7

We Must First Believe

If you can believe, all things are possible to him who believes.

—MARK 9:23

DR. BILLY GRAHAM has traveled as an evangelist to many countries in the world and says that wherever he has gone he has found people who believe there must be a God, a Supreme Being, a Creator. Both here at home and around the world, people worship God in different ways. There are many religions. But the Bible tells us there is only one true God, and that we are to believe in Him, love Him, and follow His commandments. We are also to believe in His Son, Jesus Christ, and that only through Him can we come to the Father and experience eternal life (John 14:6).

Charles Sawyer believes. Tall and stately, with hair white as snow, he welcomes guests of the Billy Graham Training Center who come to be taught the Bible. This beautiful Christian retreat in the Smoky Mountains of western North Carolina is very near the place Charlie was born eighty-two years ago. When Charlie, with his usual wide grin and warm handshake, greeted Sylvia and me on one particular October morning, I asked him what led to his position as "official greeter" at the Billy Graham Center.

A "People Person" for God

Charlie thought for a moment, widened his grin, and said,

> Even as a small boy, I guess I was a "people person." From the time I started school I always had lots of friends. In fact, four of my school chums were as close to me as family. Hubert Garrison, James Roberts, Kenneth Buckner, Fred Davis, and I were classmates all the way from grade school to high school graduation. World War II was just beginning when we graduated from Weaverville High School, and feeling a responsibility to serve our country all five of us enlisted in the Marine Corps. Hubert, James, and I had our training at Camp Pendleton in California and then were sent to the Pacific. Kenneth and Fred trained at a different boot camp before also being assigned to duty in the South Pacific fighting the Japanese.
>
> Our unit was assigned to take Saipan in the Marianna Islands. The three of us landed together under heavy Japanese artillery fire. I was knocked to the ground by exploding shells but managed to crawl under a tree along with Hubbie and Jimmy. Then a terrible thing happened. An enemy artillery shell landed right where we were, and they were both killed right next to me.

Charlie Sawyer paused for a moment while his teary eyes seemed to be looking far away and long ago. Continuing on he said,

The battle for Saipan lasted twenty-eight days, and on two more occasions I narrowly escaped injury and death. Freddie Davis, one of my other buddies from Weaverville, was not so fortunate. While fighting with his unit on Saipan, he was killed by enemy fire.

After securing Saipan, we invaded Tinian Island, captured it, and then moved on to Iwo Jima. I was wounded on the seventh day of that bloody battle when a Japanese shell exploded in the hole in which five other guys and I had taken cover. Three of my friends were killed instantly. The other two were critically wounded. The injury I suffered was from shrapnel and the concussion of the explosion. By then I was having a pretty hard time dealing with the loss of so many close friends and being wounded myself. Then I learned that Kenny Buckner, my only remaining childhood buddy, had also been killed at Iwo Jima. I was overwhelmed with sadness.

Eight months later they gave me a medical discharge from the marines, and I went home. After about a year of rehabilitation, I met, fell in love with, and married Maxine, the most wonderful girl in the world. I went to work in sales for a steel company in Asheville, North Carolina, and soon became a vice president.

For thirty-eight years I worked hard for that company, but because of poor management it went bankrupt, and I ended up with no retirement benefits. Looking back on the terrible memories of the war and experiencing the depression of having lost my retirement benefits, I became bitter. During my years in sales, entertaining customers, and keeping up of friendships, I had considered myself a social drinker. But due to my bitterness, I turned to the bottle thinking it would help me escape the painful feelings that had begun to overwhelm me. Then one day, when things had gotten really bad, a glorious thing happened: I heard God's voice speaking to me. It wasn't an audible voice, but I felt the Lord was tapping me on the shoulder to make sure He had my attention, so I stopped and listened to Him. He said, "Charlie, you're kidding yourself, and your behavior isn't being fair to your family. Throw down that bottle and get on My team." Right then and there I got down on my knees and asked God for His forgiveness for the sins in my life. He did forgive me, and with His help I haven't touched a drop of liquor in eighteen years.

My wonderful wife, Maxine, and I have been married for fifty-seven years now. We have a lovely daughter in Atlanta, Georgia, and a wonderful son in Miami, Florida. He's a minister primarily serving Spanish-speaking people. He and our daughter-in-law have five children who grew up mostly in Spain and Ecuador so they have a special heart for the world. Maxine and I really feel blessed by our children and grandchildren.

I've been a member of Weaverville Presbyterian Church for sixty-seven years, and on Sunday you will find me there, singing in the choir. But I know being a church member doesn't automatically make a person a Christian. When I got around to listening to what God was saying to me, and then rededicated my life to His service, my life became new again. Part of having that new life was finally being able to deal with the question I had asked myself over and over again for all those years: Why, Lord? Why did Hubbie and Jimmy, Kenny and Freddie lose their lives over there in the Pacific fighting in a war in our dangerous world, and You allowed me to come back home again? Why have You blessed me so abundantly, giving me a wonderful wife, children, grandchildren, and the gift of living into my eighties and maybe beyond?

I finally realized the answer was that God still had work for me to do for Him. About that time, thirteen years ago, I heard about the new Billy Graham Training Center at the Cove. I came up here and asked them if there was something a retired vice president of a now-bankrupt steel mill might be able to do here that would make a difference in the lives of others. They said something about how good I was at meeting people and believed God wanted me to serve Him by opening the door at the main entrance, greeting people each morning and making them feel welcome here. These past thirteen years at the Cove have been the high point of my life.

Charlie Sawyer has taken the special gift God has given him as a "people person," and he uses his friendly smile to warm the hearts of others and to bring honor and glory to the Lord. Most people he welcomes at the Cove already believe; they have come to the Billy Graham Training Center to learn more about serving the Lord. But some people do come as seekers, and perhaps God uses Charlie's smile and his warm, friendly manner as the first step in opening their hearts and minds to Him. Charlie's heart is filled with love for Jesus Christ, and he has come to know that his mission field is sharing that love with others, right where he lives. If God wills it and gives him the strength and the good health to do it, he plans to be standing there at the Cove, opening that door for others every morning for the rest of his life.

God has called Charles Sawyer to show His love for others. He considers himself wonderfully blessed in having been given this opportunity to give to others in this way. Charlie has said to the Lord, "Yes, Lord, I'll go; send me. I'll go up to the Cove at six o'clock each morning and open the door for people on your behalf, knowing that is what You have called me to do."

A RICH POOR MAN

Several thousand miles away, Jim Pattison also knows God has called him to fulfill a mission with the living of his life. Jim used to be a used-car salesman in Vancouver, British Columbia. Today he is one of Canada's wealthiest men, a remarkable achievement for an only child of a struggling young couple who lost everything they had in the Great Depression of 1929.

Jimmy lived with his mother and father, Julia and Chandos Pattison, in a rented attic room in the Saskatoon, Saskatchewan, home of Mr. and Mrs. Priol. The Pattisons paid rent of two dollars a month for this little room, furnished only with a bed, a table, a single chair, a small coal and wood stove, and a little cot for Jimmy. The only clothes the family had were hand-me-downs.

Because of the great hardships, Chandos Pattison had experienced, gambling and drinking had become a big part of his life. One cold, blustery night, as more snow was beginning to fall, he walked the streets of Saskatoon in despair. Passing a Pentecostal church, he heard music coming from the evening worship service inside. Wanting to get out of the snow and warm himself, he went inside the church and sat in the back row. The preacher was telling how God could change a person's life through His Son, Jesus Christ. As the pastor finished giving his message, he asked people to come forward if they wanted their lives to change. Chandos had been sitting with his head bowed, thinking about how his life was in a shambles. When the invitation was given, he found himself getting up and going forward to accept Jesus Christ as his Lord and Savior.

Jim Pattison says,

> Looking back now I realize that my dad became a changed man that evening. After his experience he started straightening his life out. Dad moved us to Vancouver where he was blessed in finding work going door to door demothing pianos. Later he was able to get a job as a used-car salesman, and eventually became sales manager for the Packard dealership in Vancouver. He worked daytime selling cars, but six nights every week he went down to Vancouver's skid row to work at a Pentecostal gospel mission to help others. In the process he was able to share the gospel, and God changed the lives of many as they came to know His Son, Jesus Christ.
>
> My dad lived twenty-eight more years after coming to know Jesus Christ as Lord and Savior. When he died, he left a total estate of $3,800. In a financial sense, that was all that he had to show for a lifetime of hard work. But at his funeral service, the church was packed with people. There wasn't a Cadillac, Mercedes, or any other make of fancy cars outside the church on that day. In fact, the parking lot was nearly empty because most of the people who attended the funeral of Chandos Pattison came on the bus. These were people who didn't have much in this life, but every one of them felt rich because they had been blessed in knowing my dad as their friend.

On the day that Chandos Pattison went home to be with the Lord, Jim said good-bye not only to the father he loved, but to a man he greatly admired. And Chandos Pattison too would have felt very proud had he lived to see what God would lead his son to accomplish in life.

Jim and Mary Pattison have been married for nearly fifty-two years. Mary was at Jim's side when he was a used-car salesman, and she is at his side now as he heads the far-flung business interests of the Jim Pattison Group, a company that the Lord allowed him the opportunity to build from the ground up. One of their projects has been the Pacific Academy. Their personal thirty-five million dollars funded the large Christian school in Surrey, British Columbia, built for educating and training Christian young people to be world leaders.

Today, many people know Jim Pattison's name because of his great success in the business world. Only close friends have known the story of Chandos Pattison and how his decision to trust Jesus Christ as Lord and Savior, led Jim on an amazing journey of extraordinary success in life.

Jim and Mary have never forgotten their roots or their love for the Lord. On Sunday mornings they are in church, and the work they do reflects their strong Christian faith. Through their commitment to share God's love and the resources He has blessed them with, they have been able to make a difference by giving help to countless people who are in need, leading them to believe in a loving God.

The Tommy Coomes Band provides music at Franklin Graham festivals and Billy Graham missions. One number they sing contains these lyrics: "He knows my name. He knows my every thought. He sees each tear that falls, and hears me when I call."[1]

On that cold, wintry night in Saskatoon many years ago, God

knew Chandos Pattison's name. He knew Chandos Pattison's every thought, and He saw each tear that fell as a defeated and lost Chandos Pattison sat in the back pew of that Pentecostal church. When Chandos called out to the Lord in anguish and despair because of the sense of failure he was feeling, God heard his call and lifted him up and gave him new birth and new life.

When Charlie Sawyer felt overwhelmed by his feelings of the loss of his four closest childhood friends, God knew his pain. When he lost his retirement income and began to experience the sadness of growing older and of no longer feeling there was a purpose for his life, God knew his name and heard his cry for help. Charlie heard God's voice, and he responded to God's call to serve Him by saying, "Yes, Lord, use me."

Charlie Sawyer and Chandos Pattison both grew up believing in God, but it was not until they felt overwhelmed and defeated by life's adversities that they were brought to their knees, and in prayer turned their lives over to Him. Then God blessed them both, leading them to begin to *live* in ways they had never imagined before.

A Special Talent to Get Things Done

It was different with Ken Isaacs. He came to believe and accept Jesus Christ as his Lord and Savior when he was a boy of twelve. After graduation from high school he went to work for a water-well drilling company in the mountains of western North Carolina. Ken not only loved his work drilling for water, he also fell in love with and married the boss's beautiful daughter, Carolyn.

After Ken completed two short-term assignments as a volunteer worker in West Africa, he and Carolyn started to pray that God would lead them in finding a way in which they could serve Him overseas as missionaries. After seventeen months of praying about this, and realizing they had no special training or formal education, they gave up their dream, believing God had answered their prayers with a no. Then God's answer came in a way they could never have imagined possible.

A friend introduced Ken to a young man named Franklin Graham, who wanted to have a well dug at his farm home. Ken remembers saying to him one day, "Franklin, if anything ever comes up concerning finding water in places where you are doing work in Africa, please let me know." Sometime later Franklin took Ken up on his offer, asking him if he would be willing to go to Ethiopia to explore the possibility of drilling water wells in that country as part of a missions program. Ken and Carolyn prayed about Franklin's request for six weeks or more before telephoning him to say, "Yes, we'll go." Ken now says of their decision, "Sometimes I look back on that period of prayer and closeness to the Lord and realize the way He raised me up, literally from the mud as a blue-collar well driller. Then He led me to do work for His glory in countries around the world. I feel greatly humbled by the way He has blessed Carolyn and me."

When Ken and Carolyn Isaacs went to Ethiopia to serve the Lord, that country was in its seventeenth year of a war that had resulted in the death of over one million people. Through their faithful work in that war-torn country, they were able to show the *love* of Jesus Christ and to *give* to thousands of people the wonderful blessing of pure, clean, crystal-clear drinking water. Through establishing a full-fledged water-well drilling program for the National Evangelical Church, and through their Christian witness at Ethiopia's Kale Heywet Church, Ken and Carolyn were able to lead others to *believe* in a loving God. And because of their time in Ethiopia their own lives were forever changed.

I first met Ken Isaacs in Moscow in August 1991 while in that city with Franklin for the Billy Graham School of Evangelism in the Lenin Sports Complex. On an earlier visit there, we had identified the need for medical equipment and supplies, and through Samaritan's Purse a new x-ray machine and other medical equipment had been shipped to Moscow. Franklin had brought Ken to Moscow to handle the logistics of getting these items through Russian customs so they could be presented to the five thousand pastors and church leaders who would be attending the meetings. These were people who had come from across the far expanse of the former Soviet Union to hear God's Word and to pray for His leading of their country.

Ken Isaacs appeared tired and somewhat exasperated when I met him that first evening in Moscow. He greeted Franklin and me by saying, "I have spent eleven hours in this big customs warehouse, just getting permission to move this x-ray machine and the other crates and boxes from that corner to this corner! The rules and regulations and red tape here are unbelievable!"

Franklin responded, "Ken, the important thing is that you got it done. And it's going to be a real expression of God's love for the Russian people when we are able to stand on that stage this evening and present this stuff to those five thousand pastors."

Ken Isaacs is a very bright, hardworking, persistent individual who loves the Lord and knows how to get things done. A German industrialist friend of mine once shared a saying with me that illustrates the special talent Ken has for being able to get things done: "He knows where on the wall the door is cut." This quality is not learned at great colleges and universities, but from experiences of living on the front lines of daily life—experiences like drilling wells.

Over the course of the past fifteen years, Ken Isaacs has been given greater and greater responsibility at Samaritan's Purse, and he is now the international director of projects, overseeing work for Franklin and Samaritan's Purse in more than one hundred countries around the world. Wherever there are sick and injured people, Franklin feels the heartbeat of the need, has the vision for the way to respond, and then sends Ken to carry out the project.

As international director of projects, Ken is involved in work in nearly one hundred different countries. One of the countries that is especially close to Franklin's heart is war-torn Southern Sudan, where he first sent Ken in February 1993. Ken describes it this way:

> I saw incredible suffering at the village of Ulang. Daytime temperatures reached 130 degrees. The flies were so thick they almost covered people's faces, contributing to the spread of diseases. The general health situation was extremely bad, and people were suffering from malnutrition. After ten days in Ulang, we had to be evacuated because the area was overrun by soldiers of opposing armies.
>
> In April 1997 Franklin had me return to Southern Sudan. This time our small missionary airplane flew at an altitude of only two hundred feet to avoid detection by soldiers of the National Islamic Front who waited to shoot us down. The local "hospital" in Mundri was a bombed-out building where about sixty wounded, dying Sudanese were lying on the concrete floor. They were being cared for by a man with no medical training, but he was the closest thing to a nurse they had. Outside the building, bloodstained bandages taken from patients who had died were washed and then laid on the grass to dry in the hot sun before being used again for other patients.
>
> Back in Nairobi, Franklin instructed our Samaritan's

Purse staff to assemble and fill several footlockers with medications and bandages. These were then flown to Mundri so we could begin our medical relief program.

I received permission to cross the river to the village of Lui, where I saw bodies of fallen soldiers still lying in the trenches and on the roads. My stomach was turned by the overwhelming stench of death that surrounded me, and my heart was broken. I will never forget seeing casualties of war lying on the floor of bombed-out buildings. Yet in spite of their infected wounds, great pain, and the foul smell of their broken bodies, the patients had strength in their suffering that would be impossible for a Westerner to understand. No one cried out in pain; the injured seldom even moaned.

Lui was once a large village. We were told that a Scottish missionary named Dr. Kenneth Fraser and his wife had come to Lui in the 1920s and had built a thriving hospital there. Now the hospital was a decaying building in the middle of a minefield. Dr. Frazer's body lay buried next to the church nearby. The plight of the thirty to forty Sudanese people who still lived in Lui and the surrounding countryside made me want to cry. This terrible war that had brought death and suffering to this area, was not over religion or even ethnic hatred. It was about oppression and the struggle of innocent people to experience freedom. I couldn't get the suffering of the people out of my mind.

Franklin saw a great opportunity for bringing help to them and asked me to return to the Sudan to further assess the situation and develop a projcct plan. Arriving back in Lui in July, I met with village leaders of the Episcopal

Church of Sudan and representatives of the Sudan Relief and Rehabilitation Agency. For three days we sat under a large tree named "the slave tree," the site where slaves used to be bought and sold and sometimes hanged. We discussed what Samaritan's Purse might be able to do to bring critically needed help along with the love of Jesus Christ and His gospel to the people in that area. On the third day we came to an agreement. Samaritan's Purse would open a hospital in Lui with the understanding that it would be operated as an evangelical Christian hospital, proclaiming the gospel of Jesus Christ in Word and deed.

One of the men got up, ran off to the village, and returned with a vintage Royal typewriter—with a ribbon only twenty-four inches long. I sat under the slave tree, typing on an old typewriter, using that short, worn-out ribbon over and over again until the one-page agreement was completed. We all signed, and Lui Hospital was started.

Franklin had us start the hospital in an abandoned girls' school since the old hospital building had been surrounded by land mines. In the beginning it was necessary to perform surgery under flashlights, but later we were able to install generator-powered electric operating room lights. Heat, flies, and the constant threat of attack by the Sudanese government forces from the north make work difficult even today.

Our Samaritan's Purse medical and ministry teams have grown in numbers and the Lord has abundantly blessed His work at Lui Hospital. In 1998 the old hospital site was demined, and patients from the temporary girls' school were moved to the rebuilt Lui Hospital building.

But in March 2000, the bombings by the Sudanese government forced staff and ambulatory patients to seek shelter in the caves nearby. In spite of the dangers and the threats, the work by Samaritan's Purse at Lui Hospital has progressed over the past six years. Our outreach has also expanded to the Nuba Mountains, where Sudanese Christians and Muslims are being severely persecuted. We are now involved with schools, agriculture, and emergency feeding programs, and each activity is being done in the name of Christ. Franklin has now started a second hospital in the village of Kurmuk.

Deeply committed Sudanese Christians have found hope and encouragement, as well as previously absent medical care, through the Lord's work at Lui Hospital and in other areas of Southern Sudan. We thank God for the abundant ways in which He has led and blessed the work He has called Franklin and Samaritan's Purse to do. Along with medical care and humanitarian relief to these valiant, warm, friendly, wonderful people, this work is bringing the gospel of Jesus Christ to many people who have not previously heard God's Word. As a result, many are coming to believe. And this ministry is blessing these people with God's love, bringing hope to them as they struggle against adversity.

Today the hospital in Lui is a sixty-five-bed facility with two surgical units, a nursing school, and a pediatric care center. The hospital serves a regional population of over 350,000 people, many of whom walk fifty to seventy-five miles in extreme heat and under threat of enemy forces to receive medical care. The medical staff sees an average of one hundred and fifty patients a day, seven days a week.

We live in a dangerous world, and for Sudanese Christians and non-Christians alike, Southern Sudan is one of the most dangerous places on earth. The threat posed by hostile forces from the Muslim North, and the hunger and disease that exists because of this threat, make everyday life a major challenge for these courageous people. The Bible tells us they are our neighbors, and we have been called to pray for them and bring help to them in their time of need.

Charlie Sawyer, Jim Pattison, and Ken Isaacs are as different in background, personality, talents, and professions as any three men could be. The nature of the work they have been called to do and the places in which they do their work for the Lord could not be more diverse. But each of them has a common, all-encompassing love for God and also for their neighbors. Each has a desire to give his life in service to others, leading them to believe in God and to come to Him through His Son, Jesus Christ.

Charlie Sawyer is a "people person" who serves the Lord where he was born and where he has lived his entire life. Jim Pattison is a man of vision, a deal maker in the world of big business, but he and his wife, Mary, commit a large portion of the fruits of their labors to helping others, supporting the Lord's work through a number of Christian organizations. Ken Isaacs is an organizer and a facilitator. He is able to identify what needs to be done and to see that it is accomplished. The work each of these men does is accomplished for the honor and the glory of God.

Each of these men is absolutely unique as a human being and as a child of God. And the wonderful thing is that He has made you and me just as unique, and He has a plan and a purpose for your life and mine. The Bible tells us that He is calling us to make a difference.

Before you turn the page, ask yourself these questions:

- What are the special talents that God has given to me?
- Am I achieving my greatest potential for serving Him?
- Am I living my life each day in a way that is leading others to believe?

chapter 8

Then Lead Others to Believe

But without faith it is impossible to please Him, for he who comes to God must believe that He is, and that He is a rewarder of those who diligently seek Him.

—HEBREWS 11:6

MANY PEOPLE have not had the blessing of growing up in a Christian home and are not believers in God and His Son, Jesus Christ. Many identify themselves as atheists, agnostics, or of another faith. Some even have feelings of animosity toward those who do believe in Jesus Christ as God's Son. Brent Smith was one of these people.

From the time of his childhood, Brent Smith never wanted to be anything but a cowboy. He rides his horse fifty or more miles on many working days as he herds cattle on his Nevada ranch. In his ten-gallon hat, range shirt, blue jeans, leather chaps, boots and spurs, Cowboy Brent looks all business, with plenty of meanness to back it up. His small, round, metal-rimmed glasses sit well down his nose, and there is a questioning squint to his eyes as he peers over them.

Brent speaks with a deep, gravelly voice through slightly parted lips that are partially hidden by a white, bushy, handlebar mustache. When he speaks, you know immediately he is not someone you want to cross. Those Brent Smith calls "friend" know he is a gentle soul, unless someone calls him a coward—this label is a fighting word to Cowboy Brent. More than a few men have felt the pain of Brent's lightning-fast clenched fists and now have crooked noses and scars because they made the mistake of calling him a coward.

Cowboy Brent tells his story this way:

> I came off the land. I knew there was a God because of the things around me. Calves being born, grass coming back every spring, the blustery harshness of winter, the calm beauty of summer, the dependability of the sunrise each morning, and the awesome splendor of sunset at the end of each day.
>
> I ran away from home when I was four because I didn't want to be told what to do by anybody! My parents found me and brought me back. Even as a boy, I learned to distrust and dislike most men because they didn't speak the truth, and I didn't want to be like them or around them. I searched for truth in great books, and I even tried to read the Bible but abandoned that because it was a shoe that just didn't fit. People branded me a rebel, a malcontent, a misfit who was always in trouble. I was barely thirteen years old when I got shot the first time. Always a wanderer and a drifter, I longed to see what was over the next hill, and every time what I found there was only disappointment. My granddaddy said I was independent and restless, "like a hog on ice," and I guess that summed me up pretty well.
>
> As I drifted across most of the West, breaking horses

and being a cowboy, it seemed trouble and violence followed me everywhere I went. I had heard that bad people go to hell and thought that was probably the way it should be, and I always figured that I would go to hell some day and end up riding on the devil's herd.

Then I met a special girl on a blind date. Janet was the first Christian girl I had ever met. There was something different about her, and I loved her from the first moment I met her. I didn't know how to deal with this emotion of loving someone; it went against everything I had always worked hard to avoid. My feelings for Janet made me want to warn her about the trouble and the violence I had known in my life and that I was a heavy drinker. Somehow Janet could see something she liked about me and we fell in love and got married going on forty-four years ago. Then I found out she was one of those Bible readers, one of those people who had "got religion," and I didn't have time for things like that. It was my feeling that "coming to believe" was only for cowards, and there was no way I was ever going to carry that brand!

The love Janet felt for me had no bounds. She tried many ways to share God's love with me and tell me about His Son, Jesus Christ. She prayed for me and turned our house into a Bible bookstore. It seemed there was a Bible everywhere I turned, all with the pages opened to some verse she wanted me to read. There was no way a man filled with pride like me was going to admit to reading that stuff, but when Janet wasn't looking I did read passages in her Bibles.

I had never viewed the Bible as God's Word, so when, for the first time, I began to understand the power of God Almighty, it overwhelmed me. But one thing that really bothered me in reading the stories in the Bible was how cowardly a lot of the men in those stories had been. I began to think how disappointed in mankind God must be as a result of finding He had a bunch of cowards in His outfit. I had never seen such a sorry mess.

Then one night when Janet wasn't looking I came across a passage in Isaiah 52:14 that stopped me dead in my tracks. It was a prophecy of what Christ would look like on the cross, and it got me to thinking about the unspeakable evil of the Crucifixion that came later and caused me to have a hunger in my heart to know this person, Jesus.

For a long time after that I kept on drinking, kept on fighting, and kept on searching for meaning for my life. Then one morning Janet opened the Bible and laid it on the table, and I had a look at the words written there. It was the twenty-first chapter of Revelation, and in verse eight it seemed to me what God was saying would indicate I was a coward! That really upset me, because nobody has ever called me a coward without my having a fight with him. The thought of being a coward in God's eyes really bothered me.

Then, a few days later, I was coming in from the range. As I got off my horse I just went to my knees and began weeping like a child. I said to God, "Please don't let me die a coward in Your eyes." In that moment I realized it was this Jesus that I had been searching for all my life, and I begged Him for forgiveness of my sins. Then I felt I was able to hear God's voice saying to me, "I will lead, you follow." Still on my knees I said, "I surrender."

Brent Smith is a new cowboy who is powerfully committed to sharing his faith with others. On most days he still rides his horse from sunrise to sunset herding cattle on his ranch. But there are many weeks when he is serving the Lord at Franklin Graham festivals, Billy Graham missions, and conferences at the Cove as well as at other Christian meetings and events across the country. He tells his story, gives his personal testimony, and calls upon others to follow his example by making a decision for Jesus.

When Janet met Brent Smith all those years ago, she came to love him totally and completely, just as God loves us. In spite of all of Brent's sins and shortcomings, she was able to see the good that was inside him. She was patient as she led him to give up his sinful behavior and to let the good in his heart shine forth. Even when it seemed unlikely that Brent Smith would ever change his heart, Janet never gave up on him, just as God doesn't ever give up on us. Janet made herself an example of Christian living and was persistent in leading Brent to seek answers through God's Word. Eventually Brent came to know the truth, and his life was changed.

In addition to giving his Christian witness at meetings, Cowboy Brent Smith has an active prison ministry. When he visits those who have been incarcerated, they identify with him because he has also served time in prison. When he tells about the trouble he once got into, heads all over the room nod with understanding because those prisoners know Brent has been where they currently are. Some ask for prayer, and many make decisions for Christ.

Peaceful Prisoners

I have been in prison twice, not as a prisoner but as a visitor. The first time was when I was fourteen years old. My parents and I visited the Colorado State Prison in Canyon City while on vacation. I will never forget the sound of the prison door slamming shut with a heavy, metal thud, and the loud *click* of the closing lock. My second prison visit was in 1998 to the Central Prison in Kigali, the capital city of Rwanda. More than ten thousand men and women were incarcerated, most charged with murder and genocide during the war between the Tutsi and the Hutu tribes. This bloody war of ethnic cleansing claimed the lives of an estimated eight hundred thousand people, many killed by blows from machetes.

I was in Kigali on five occasions for Samaritan's Purse, once during the war and four times after in reference to the humanitarian relief work being done under Franklin's leadership. During the last trip, I was invited to the prison to deliver a message during the weekly chapel service held there. Arriving at the main entrance to the large, high-walled prison, I was told for security reasons not to make eye contact with the prisoners. The guards also told me there were so many prisoners crowded into the facility that many filled the hallways and courtyards as well as the cells, and we would need to make our way through their tightly packed ranks.

When the guards opened the fourteen-foot-tall metal doors of the prison and we walked inside, I found myself surrounded by a throng of men, many charged with murder. And then I heard the familiar, very loud *click* that I remembered from my tour of the Colorado State Prison years before. The heavy prison gate was locked shut. All around me were Hutu and Tutsi prisoners, dressed in bright pink prison clothing to make it easier to track them down and recapture them should they escape. As we walked through the mass of men I could feel the heat and perspiration from their bodies against mine. The expression on the face of most of these men appeared to be one of meanness and evil.

After making our way through the crowded prison courtyard we came to the place where the worship service was to be held. It was a room about the size of a basketball court with brick walls at the front, back, and along one side and a sloping tin roof above. Heavy chicken wire formed a barrier on the remaining side. Prisoners who had come to attend the church service were already taking their seats on long, white benches that filled the room. Within a few minutes, approximately one thousand men had filed into the hot, tin-roofed room in which there seemed to be no air moving. Even though the room appeared packed, body against body, guards instructed the men to push even closer together to create additional space across the front of the room. Then a side door was opened and about one hundred and fifty women, some holding small babies, were led in filling the space cleared for them.

The prison chaplains made announcements, the steel drummers played, songs were sung, and then I was introduced to bring the message. As a text I used Genesis 22, the record of Abraham and his son Isaac. I spoke of Abraham's obedience to God—how he followed God's instructions to take his son Isaac to a place called Moriah and to slay him there with a knife, sacrificing him as a burnt offering. I began to feel I should have chosen a different text. Many of these prisoners were charged with genocide, knives having been used as the instrument of death! But the point of the text was how God had tested Abraham and then blessed him for his obedience, sparing the life of his son Isaac. The prisoners seemed to understand the message, and I gave thanks to the Lord for this.

Looking out upon the sea of faces of prisoners who had come for the worship service, I realized there was something wonderfully different about them. These men and women appeared to have turned their backs upon hatred and evil, and they were approaching God for forgiveness. The decisions they had made to accept Christ could be seen in the glow of peacefulness and warmth in their faces, qualities missing from the prisoners I had seen in the courtyard.

We live in a time when the seeds of hatred between tribes,

clans, countries, and peoples of different religious faiths have led to the persecution, suffering, and death of millions of people. A time when people strap heavy vests filled with explosives and nails to their bodies and blow themselves up in crowded places as an expression of their hatred for others. A time when people ask, "What is going on in the world?"

A few months ago, I was seated at a table for eight at a dinner meeting. A woman from the Middle East seated next to me said, "My heart would be filled with joy, and I would feel ultimate fulfillment as a mother if I could stand next to the coffin of my son knowing he had died a martyr for Islam. I can imagine no greater happiness than would be mine as I would pull the flag of our country down and look upon his face."

A chill passed through my body. I thought of our two sons and daughter and the way they feel called to *give* of their talents by serving others in the Lord's name. Michael, the oldest, is a trauma surgeon. He has chosen to be a doctor, bringing compassionate care and healing to others. Elizabeth is a committed Christian homemaker, a wife, and a mother. She has been very active in crisis pregnancy work through a Right to Life organization. Bob, our younger son, is a fundraising consultant, using his considerable talents to raise funds for evangelical Christian organizations. As a Christian, and as a father, I find it impossible to understand how a mother could experience fulfillment through seeing her child become a terrorist, killing innocent people.

Accounts of robberies, looting, oppression, and all manners of atrocities against others have become commonplace, and that calls us as believers in Jesus Christ to stand up and be counted in His service. Too many people are like a woman Sylvia and I visited who commented, "With all of the terrible things going on in the world today, I just 'turn it off and shut it out.' When I see accounts of wars and hunger and needy people, I just go on channel surfing until I find some sports program or something else fun to watch." She knew of our work through Samaritan's Purse and the Billy Graham Evangelistic Association, and perhaps for this reason she added, "I don't believe in God. If there really is a God, why is He letting all these terrible things happen to people? I choose to believe in nature and in enjoying life. I don't bother other people, and don't want them bothering me. Anyway, *why believe?* If there is a God, and He is a loving God as you say He is, then when I die He sure isn't going to do anything bad to me—especially nothing like throwing me into the fire in a place called hell!"

In his excellent book entitled *Why Believe*, pastor Greg Laurie has addressed this question. He admits that he was at best a token believer: "Oh, I believed there was a God up there somewhere. At least I believed enough to remember to say, 'God help me,' when I was in trouble or when I wanted something. But as far as having a relationship with God and really believing He knew I was there and that He cared for me, there was none of that."[1] But then Greg went through a period of loneliness in his life, feeling an emptiness that needed to be filled. Following the lead taken by a girl he admired, he made his decision to accept Jesus Christ as Lord and Savior. Today Greg is senior pastor at Harvest Christian Fellowship in Riverside, California, and a well-known evangelist.

My first meeting with Greg was in a hotel restaurant in Costa Mesa, California, where he joined Franklin and me for lunch. He impressed me as someone exceptionally bright, very talented, and somewhat shy. I found him to be immediately likeable. After lunch, Greg kept us laughing by telling interesting stories and by drawing caricatures of famous people. I remember telling him I thought he could have found great success drawing professionally.

Later, we heard Greg preach at the Harvest Crusade at Anaheim Stadium. I was amazed by the way God spoke through him with a simplicity and a clarity of the gospel message that led many to understand God's Word and to respond to His call by coming forward when the invitation was given.

Since that time a number of years ago I have had the special blessing of coming to know Greg and his wife, Cathe, as friends, and I have served with Greg on the boards of both the Billy Graham Evangelistic Association and Samaritan's Purse. One story Greg has shared on a number of occasions is the way Dr. Billy Graham has impacted his life. Greg has said, "I used to dream of someday standing in a crowd and being able to reach out and shake the hand of Billy Graham as he passed by. The idea of actually meeting him seemed so remote that it never entered my mind. But it happened, and the Lord blessed me in becoming his friend, even going to his home to sit and talk and share a meal with him at his table. And now having the blessing of serving on his board of directors is something I never could have imagined."

This story reminds us that Jesus told His disciples, "I have called you friends . . ." (John 15:15). Through *believing* in Jesus Christ and following in His footsteps, we are able to know Him as "friend." We are given the blessing of being able to sit with Him at His table and the privilege of serving with Him. Through our friendship with Jesus, we are able to experience wonderful blessings that we never could have imagined before.

Pastor Greg Laurie is being led by the Lord to blaze the trail of preaching the gospel in our time. He is doing this not only through his ministry at Harvest Christian Fellowship in Riverside, California, but also through radio and television ministry, books, and Harvest Crusades held across the United States and overseas. On the very day I wrote his story, I knew Greg was flying from California to

Australia to begin a Harvest Crusade there. And I knew that Skip Heitzig had just returned to his ministry as senior pastor at the fourteen-thousand member Calvary Chapel Albuquerque, having just preached to thousands of people in Singapore.

Tried It All; Chose God

Like Greg, Skip Heitzig grew up with a marginal belief in God and certainly with no real commitment to ever believe otherwise. And like Greg, Skip's early years were lived in the fast-moving Orange County, California, of the 1960s and 1970s. Skip tried all kinds of different things in his search for truth and meaning for his life, even venturing into the occult and experimenting with drugs. During Skip's early years, his burning ambition was to become a doctor. But becoming a CT scan technician was as close as he came to achieving that dream.

As a tall, good-looking, charming guy with a motorcycle, surfboard, and guitar, Skip was never short on friends. In the hang-loose-and-stay-free culture of Southern California during the years of his youth, meaning and pleasure in his life were always "just a snort away." Skip loved having a good time, and like most young people he had no fears and perhaps even believed he would somehow live forever.

One evening at the age of seventeen he arrived back at his apartment somewhat stoned and worn out. Kicking off his shoes, he sat down to do some channel surfing on television. After clicking past several stations he went back to one and found it was Billy Graham.

All day Skip Heitzig had been surrounded by the noise of his fast-moving life: the pounding surf, the roar of his motorcycle, and meaningless laughter. The blare of the music at the disco where he had stayed far too long, and the noise created by other people all seeking earthly pleasures in an attempt to fill the voids in their lives, had finally worn him down. At last it was quiet, except for the voice of Dr. Billy Graham, who was nearing the end of his message. When Dr. Graham give the invitation that night, Skip Heitzig accepted Jesus Christ as his Lord and Savior, doing so right in front of his television set.

In the time that followed, Skip began to use his time and his talents more wisely and fully. He studied at Trinity Seminary, earning both bachelor's and master's degrees. He also studied under Pastor Chuck Smith at Calvary Chapel in Costa Mesa, California. Then in 1982 Skip and his wife, Lenya, felt called to go to Albuquerque, New Mexico, where they gathered a few people together in their home for a Bible study. From that simple beginning the Lord has raised up the large Calvary Chapel Albuquerque, a ministry that continues to grow and to reach out to the world, making a difference.

I am privileged to serve with Skip on the board of Samaritan's Purse and to know him as a close and valued friend. Opportunities to hear him teach from God's Word are always memorable because of the clarity with which he explains the meaning of the Scriptures and the way he makes God's Word so relevant to life in our time. But before hearing God's call to ministry, Skip's job called for him to use a CT scanner to look inside patients' bodies, providing answers for them concerning what was wrong in their lives physically. Now Skip uses his God-given talents and his study time to look inside the words of Scripture to provide answers for people concerning what is wrong in their lives spiritually.

Skip and Lenya made the difficult decision to leave the work they had started in Albuquerque twenty-three years ago moving in January 2004 to San Juan Capistrano, California. As Senior Pastor of Ocean Hills Church Skip has already seen attendance triple in the first two months of his ministry. Skip and Lenya are truly making a difference for God's glory.

Three evangelists, all nonbelievers, or at best nominal believers during an earlier time in their lives. Each one heard God's Word and came to know Him through His Son, Jesus Christ. Each one is a committed servant leading others to believe because one other person cared enough to share the gospel with them.

Cowboy Brent Smith was led to know Jesus by his loving wife. He dragged his feet in doubt and protest every step of the way, but finally found himself on his knees in submission.

Pastor Greg Laurie was led to Christ by a girl he admired, but had only met and talked with one time. In his moment of submission, Greg responded to an unknown preacher's invitation, making his decision for Christ so fast that he found himself standing to publicly declare his faith, almost without realizing he was doing it.

Pastor Skip Heitzig found the answers he was seeking in life through a brief and simple message on television, presented by the son of a dairy farmer from North Carolina named Billy Graham. As he was led by God to this encounter with truth, Skip was brought to his knees in submission, experiencing a change in his life so remarkable that his testimony has become an inspiration drawing countless others to Jesus Christ.

Before you turn the page, ask yourself these questions:

- What about me? Do I truly believe, and can others see this in my life?
- Have I told anyone else about Jesus Christ in order that they might believe?
- Am I prepared to make a difference by living my life in the Lord's service?

chapter 9

God's Plan for Those who Believe

And this is His commandment: that we should believe on the name of His Son Jesus Christ and love one another, as He gave us commandment.

—1 JOHN 3:23

IT WAS OCTOBER 19, 1989, and Sylvia and I were in Berlin, Germany, waiting to meet a man we had long admired. When he walked into the room, I was impressed by Dr. Billy Graham's warm and friendly manner as he extended his hand to shake mine. Then Dr. Graham graciously thanked me for serving alongside Franklin at Samaritan's Purse. As we sat and talked together I found Dr. Billy Graham to be the same person I had seen so many times on television and had imagined he would be.

Dr. Graham invited Sylvia, our son Robert and me to accompany him and Billy Graham Evangelistic Association team members as they drove into East Berlin that evening for a meeting of church leaders and pastors. The purpose of the meeting was to pray for the Billy Graham crusade to be held the next afternoon on the steps of the historic Reichstag. It was bitterly cold as we passed through Checkpoint Charlie and then drove through the darkened streets of East Berlin. Reunification of the two Germanys had not yet taken place, but the Berlin Wall was already being torn down, and earlier that day we had been able to take our turn swinging sledgehammers to bring this about.

We arrived at the large Gethsemane Lutheran Church to find it packed with one thousand or more pastors and church leaders. As Rev. Billy Graham entered the large sanctuary and stepped to the podium, all of those assembled stood out of respect and applauded.

Then Billy Graham said something like this:

> Thank you. I feel deeply honored and blessed to be here with you this evening at Gethsemane Church in East Berlin. I know many of you have suffered greatly during the past many years, in part because of your trust in God. Standing here before you now is a very humbling experience for me. I want to invite you to join me in this moment by bowing your head in prayer. I feel humbled before Almighty God, and right now I want to recommit my life to Him. If you will join with me in recommitting your life to Him, as we open our hearts in prayer, I invite you to hold up your hand, in order that each one of us might be counted for Him.

Someone commented later that in that moment hands went up all over that large sanctuary as pastors and church leaders who had lived and suffered in a long-repressed Communist society humbly surrendered themselves anew before Almighty God.

In the cold rain the following afternoon, Dr. Billy Graham stood on the steps of the Reichstag, proclaiming the gospel of Jesus

Christ in the same place where Adolph Hitler had once stood and proclaimed the beginning of the "One-Thousand-Year Reich." What Adolph Hitler arrogantly announced there lasted little more than twelve years, but crosses symbolizing the crucifixion of Jesus Christ still stand high today on the steeples of churches across Germany and around the world. Our risen Lord still lives.

I feel greatly humbled as I write this book concerning the gracious work being done by people who have responded to God's call to make a difference in our dangerous world. They faithfully serve each day by bringing help to people who are suffering and by leading them to believe in our loving God and His Son.

Over the past twenty years I have served on short-term assignments with Samaritan's Purse in many places in the world. But I am not one of those servants of Jesus Christ who has faithfully served on the front line of His work, twenty-four hours a day for months or years at a time, like many of those whose stories are told in this book. There are many people who could more appropriately write about the need to make a difference in our world today. People who could better address the dangers, the needs, and the opportunities for service and evangelism in our world today—people who have committed their full-time energies and risked their lives in showing God's love, and who have given help to those in need through compassionate ministry, leading those they serve to believe in God and in His Son, Jesus Christ. Faithful, committed servants like Dr. Richard Bransford and his wife, Millie . . . and like Karen Daniels, RN.

Nurse with Courage

Karen Daniels is a thirty-one-year-old nurse from Cranbrook, British Columbia. During the early months of 2002, she heard God's voice, calling her to respond to the need for nurses at the

Samaritan's Purse hospital at Lui, Sudan. Karen had previously served in a short-term medical mission assignment through Samaritan's Purse in the Dominican Republic, and the memories of her experiences there had never left her mind or her heart.

Karen tells her story this way:

> Following five months of preparation, I flew to Nairobi and then to Lui, arriving there in September. I had only been at Lui Hospital for a few hours when the sound of an aircraft could be heard approaching the area. Looking up, I could see it was a large airplane and thought it was probably carrying cargo. It circled overhead several times and then vanished into the distance. The next day the same airplane, a large Russian Antonov, returned to the sky over Lui. This time it passed low overhead, and we could see the tail section of the aircraft open up. As we stood watching, several large fuel drums were rolled out of the back of the airplane and began falling toward us.
>
> Realizing we were being bombed by Sudanese Army forces from the North, more senior hospital staff members began to shout, "Run! Run as fast as you can to the caves!" I joined the others and ran as fast as I could to the caves nearby to find shelter. We stayed there for over half an hour to make sure the bombing had ceased.
>
> We emerged to find the "bombs" had been petrol drums filled with gasoline and shrapnel, each set to explode upon impact. Fortunately, because of the inaccuracy of this primitive kind of bombing, the hospital was not hit and no people were killed.
>
> Two weeks later a MiG jet aircraft fired its payload on a less fortunate group of Sudanese Dinka cattle herders

from the area, and thirteen were killed including a pregnant woman and four children. In addition, twenty of the cows that meant so much to the Dinkas for supplying milk were also killed. The wounded were brought to our hospital at Lui, and one of the men I cared for had lost a leg, blown off by one of the exploding bombs.

For the first time I realized the real tragedies of a terrible war that has gone on for the past twenty years. It was hard for me to deal with this, but I found the peace I was seeking through reading Psalm 27:

> The LORD is my light and my salvation;
> Whom shall I fear?
> The LORD is the strength of my life;
> Of whom shall I be afraid?
> When the wicked came against me
> to eat up my flesh,
> My enemies and foes,
> They stumbled and fell.
> Though an army may encamp against me;
> My heart shall not fear;
> Though war may rise against me,
> In this I will be confident.
>
> —PSALM 27:1–3

Karen is a registered nurse and she has worked mainly in cancer care for the past ten years in Vancouver and Kelowna, British Columbia. It is amazing to hear her tell of her work at Lui Hospital and to realize that after completing her first year of duty, she signed up for another year of service without a moment's hesitation. Lui is a place where temperatures reach 115 degrees or more during the day and often drop to no lower than 95 degrees in the middle of the night. Lui is so isolated from every modern convenience that taking a shower means standing under a bucket with holes in the bottom, and the only "bathrooms" are latrine trenches dug in the ground, shielded by a tarpaulin hung between two poles.

Karen Daniels was one of three who chose to stay behind at Lui Hospital after the bombing. She said of her decision, "When they told me I would be getting hazardous duty pay, I had to chuckle. Samaritan's Purse was very forthright in telling me the risks should I decide to stay, but I felt that God wanted me to remain at Lui and that nothing bad would happen to me there."

Before Karen left Vancouver to fly back to Lui, her mother expressed her concern for Karen's safety but then added, "I know Karen needs to go back, because her heart is still there." Karen says of her loving, supportive mother, "She is an amazing person."

It is inspiring and challenging to hear about the things people like Karen Daniels are doing in order to make a difference in our dangerous world. They make their commitment because Jesus said, "Inasmuch as you did it unto one of the least of these My brethren, you did it to Me"(Matthew 25:40). They responded to His great commission to, "Go therefore and make disciples of all nations, baptizing them in the name of the Father and of the Son and of the Holy Spirit, and teaching them to obey everything that I have commanded you" (Matthew 28:19–20 NRSV).

Like Father, Like Son

Franklin Graham also committed his life to helping others who are hungry, thirsty, sick, or otherwise in need and has traveled the world responding in God's name to the needs of suffering humanity. But God had an even greater plan for Franklin's life than just doing Christian relief work. As with his father, Rev. Billy Graham, Franklin would be called to become an evangelist, proclaiming the gospel in the arenas and stadiums of the world. In April 1997, we were in a large soccer stadium in Johannesburg, South Africa, and Franklin had just stepped up to the microphone to preach the gospel to the forty-five thousand or more people who had come seeking answers for their questions about life. As Franklin began his message that night, my thoughts returned to the time when he had believed his calling was only to bring medical relief to people suffering in a hurting world. He had no intention of ever preaching like his father. I smiled in amazement as I observed and listened to evangelist Franklin Graham delivering a powerful gospel message to thousands of people.

Early that same morning I had eaten breakfast with Franklin and Dennis Agajanian in the coffee shop of our hotel. Later about fifty other members of the Franklin Graham festival and I met for morning devotions led by Dr. Ross Rhoads. During the prayer time that followed, Franklin knelt and led the team in praying for the Lord's blessings upon the meetings in South Africa. After Franklin finished praying, every member prayed aloud, one at a time, on his knees before Almighty God.

After the morning devotions, Franklin gave several television and radio interviews and then spoke at a luncheon hosted by prominent Johannesburg church, civic, and business leaders. In the early afternoon Franklin, his wife, Jane, recording artist Michael W. Smith, and others visited a large children's hospital located on the edge of the Soweto District of Johannesburg. As a visiting neurosurgeon I was asked to examine several children with brain tumors and explain their illness and prognosis to Franklin. In his eyes I saw his deep compassion for these little children and witnessed the empathy in his heart that I had seen there so many times before as I had traveled with him in other countries around the world.

Franklin prayed for these sick children, and then he and Jane led our team as we handed out Operation Christmas Child shoebox gifts to the little children in that hospital. In Franklin and Jane, Michael W. Smith, and other members of the Samaritan's Purse team I saw the love of Jesus Christ. This love radiated from their faces as they went from bed to bed in that children's ward, smiling and laughing and sharing the excitement of each moment while helping the children open their shoebox gifts, given as an expression of the love of Jesus Christ. This same expression of the love of Jesus Christ began to spread among doctors, nurses, and parents of the little children who were sick, extending from one ward to another as we moved around the hospital.

That afternoon Franklin spent time in Bible study and prayer with the Lord in preparation for preaching of God's Word that evening, in a stadium that would be filled with thousands of people, coming to hear a message of redemption, hope, and salvation.

Franklin has described himself as having been a rebel in his youth, living in the fast lane, chasing pleasure in search of meaning. But this man I am blessed and privileged to know as a close friend is no longer a rebel. He, like his father, is a deeply committed, obedient servant of God who has given his life to the Lord, to be used fully in service to others.

Since that Franklin Graham festival in Johannesburg, South Africa, there have been many more evangelical meetings, held in many other cities at home and around the world. The language, the culture, the food, even the color of people's skin has varied from place to place, but the gospel message has always been the same, because God does not change. Hebrews 13:8 says, "Jesus Christ is the same yesterday, today, and forever." Franklin is truly a man of God who works tirelessly in his effort to make a difference in the lives of people everywhere, bringing not just help, but hope to them.

. . . AND YOU FED ME

Sami Dagher is another friend who is working hard to make a difference in the lives of people for God's glory. Sami is a Lebanese pastor and evangelist. His life has come a long way since the days of his childhood as the youngest of seven children, born into a poor farming family in a hillside village near the ancient city of Sidon, a few miles south of Beirut, Lebanon.

From a very early age Sami Dagher had dreams of a more exciting life than he felt he could ever know in that rural farming community. In his teens he left the family farm to attend hotelier school. Then he decided to go off and see the world. After working in hotels in Turkey and Libya, Sami traveled to England and worked in a luxury hotel near Marble Arch. While in London, he met and fell in love with a beautiful English girl named Joy.

Returning to Beirut with his young bride, Sami Dagher landed a job at the famous Hotel Phoenicia and rose through the ranks to become maître d´ in that posh establishment. With his dark hair, imposing stance, winning smile, and money in his pockets, he looked the epitome of success. But Sami knew things were not right with him, and inside he had a gnawing feeling of emptiness and lack of fulfillment.

If asked his religious affiliation during those days in the hotel business, Sami Dagher would have told you he was a Christian. And this would have seemed to him a reasonable response. After all, he had come from a Lebanese Catholic family, and on Christmas and Easter he usually did go to services, and in addition he went to church for weddings, baptisms, and funerals. But the truth was he had never taken time to read the Bible or to really concern himself with spiritual matters.

As the emptiness in Sami's life continued to grow, he confided this unhappiness to a friend who suggested he talk with an American missionary couple who had recently come to Beirut. Finally, in the spring of 1967, after some time of procrastination, Sami felt broken enough in spirit that he took Joy by the hand and went for lunch with the missionary couple, Harry and Miriam Taylor, as his friend had suggested. When the Taylors opened their Bible and began to read from it, Sami and Joy could see answers to their questions.

Several months after being introduced to God's Word, both Sami and Joy made commitments to Christ and their lives began to change. Even though Sami was still working at the Phoenicia, he started to sense that he was being called into the ministry. After two years of inner struggle regarding his future, Sami finally went to the hotel's general manager to announce his resignation. The general manager was angry when he heard what Sami planned to do, and he said, "You are crazy to leave your job! You will not be able to provide for your family. If you do leave, don't come knocking on my door looking for a crust of bread, because the door will stay closed!" In spite of the doubts of friends, Sami started a Christian and Missionary Alliance church in Beirut and his ministry grew. Several years later civil war broke out in Lebanon, and the Phoenicia Hotel was destroyed by the shelling. As a result the hotel's general manager came to Sami Dagher's home one day asking for food for his family to eat. Sami gave him the help his family needed and also shared the gospel with him.

Rev. Sami Dagher has been abundantly blessed, and he is now head of the six Christian and Missionary Alliance churches in

Lebanon. He has been led by the Lord to start a Bible school that offers training for students from Jordan, Syria, Egypt, Sudan, Iraq, and Greece. He is in demand as an evangelist, preaching and teaching in the U.S. and in other countries. And several years before the fall of Saddam Hussein's regime, Sami Dagher started an evangelical Christian church in Baghdad and brought humanitarian relief assistance to people who were suffering there. I went to Baghdad with him in 2000 and saw him at work.

Sami Dagher continues to share the gospel, leading others to come to believe. He no longer experiences emptiness in his life because every moment of every day is filled with happiness, fulfillment, and excitement. He knows he is doing what God wants him to do, and that with God's leading he is able to make a difference in people's lives. The ministry of Sami Dagher is a testimony to the fact that God can take one individual who will answer His call and perform miracles through that person, as He did with a young girl who lived in Panama.

Going for the True Gold

The Panama girl's story is closely tied to an unusual man I was privileged to meet—a man who is distinguished, articulate, knowledgeable, a gifted leader and communicator, and most important of all, a man of God. Rev. A. R. Bernard Sr., is the senior pastor and founder of Christian Cultural Center in Brooklyn, New York. In 1978 he started a small, storefront church, and God has blessed it, raising it up to become a non-profit ministry with more than seventeen thousand members.

I first met Rev. Bernard at a dinner in Washington, D.C. That evening I found him to be so interesting that I didn't want to miss a single word of his riveting stories. One particular story he told really caught my attention and touched my heart in a powerful way. It was the story of the young girl from his native Panama. During the darkest hours of her life she heard God's voice and was led to believe.

As Rev. Bernard told the story:

> She was beautiful, a gifted athlete, and young. Running track for the Republic of Panama, she had already become an Olympic bronze and silver medalist in the women's relay and in the one-hundred-meter dash. She was a figure of national pride and had won a place on the Olympic team for the games in Helsinki in 1950–51. Unfortunately, political turmoil forced cancellation of Panama's participation in those games.
>
> This young runner was given a real advantage, with four more years in which to train to "go for the gold" in the next Olympic Games. Seizing upon this opportunity, she trained for hours each day at Pacific Stadium. Across the street from the stadium was a busy restaurant where she would join other young athletes to talk, laugh, and dream of the future.
>
> The owner of the restaurant showed special interest in this young, female athlete and actively pursued her. An impressionable virgin of eighteen, she was quite vulnerable and during her first sexual encounter with him, she became pregnant. When the restaurant owner found out, he was very upset and ended the relationship promptly without assuming any responsibility.
>
> For her athletic coach and the Panama Olympic Committee members, the girl's pregnancy became a big problem. They told her that allowing the pregnancy to

continue would mean losing her place on the team as well as losing a full scholarship to study at Tuskegee Institute in the United States. Some recommended that she have an abortion. She knew this would be wrong and felt compelled to allow the pregnancy to continue and then to keep her baby. The young girl understood this would mean losing everything: her chance to win the Olympic gold medal, a full scholarship to study in the U.S., and the acclaim of the people of Panama—everything but her baby.

The media was quick to report her decision to have the baby and withdraw from Olympic competition, and the response from Panamanians was overwhelmingly negative. Even her very conservative Catholic country condemned her for becoming pregnant and gave her no words of support for her decision to have the baby. Even more painful was the embarrassment her pregnancy and withdrawal from Olympic competition brought upon her family.

The day the baby was born, the young, unwed mother brought her son directly to the restaurant owner. She believed seeing the baby boy he had fathered would change his mind, and he would marry her. But he turned away, leaving her to suffer even further rejection by him.

Feeling deeply hurt and broken in spirit, she took her baby to the home of her grandmother, who was a member of the Salvation Army. Her grandmother always spoke lovingly with her about God, and she told her of God's love for her and for her baby. Then her grandmother taught her how to pray to God and how to listen for God's voice. The young mother went to her room and placed her newborn baby boy on the bed next to her. Then she wrote a short prayer and placed the folded sheet of paper in the family Bible.

That young girl from Panama, who dreamed of winning the Olympic gold medal and then became pregnant and had to withdraw was my mother! Had she chosen to have an abortion in order to compete in the Olympic Games, I wouldn't be here with you gentlemen this evening. I wouldn't be a pastor, sharing with people God's Word and leading them to come to believe in His Son, and I wouldn't be going with you to the White House for our meeting with the president of the United States tomorrow.

After three years of my mother's trying to rise above her ordeal of being an unwed mother, my uncles provided enough money to send my mother and me to the United States where she could begin a new life. My mother gave up all for me, and I love and admire her more than I can express. She didn't win the Olympic gold, but because she heard God's voice speaking to her, and because she allowed God to lead her to make the right decision, I am here today.

Several years ago, my cousin was writing a thesis about my mother and her life. While looking through my mother's Bible, she found the prayer written by her all those years ago. My mother's prayer was this: "Lord, I was a household name, and I gave it all up to have this baby. I pray that one day this baby will pick up where I left off."

When he was four, A.R. Bernard's mother brought him to New York City and established a home for them in the Bedford-Stuyvesant section of Brooklyn. Life was not easy for Ms. Bernard as a single parent, and at an early age A. R. worked at low-paying jobs in the garment district. As a high school senior he started a job in the Consumer Lending Division at Bankers Trust Company, where eventually he became an operations specialist. At age twenty-five, he felt the call to full-time ministry and with his wife, Karen, started a Bible study group in their home. Later it was moved to the storefront building in Brooklyn. Rev. Bernard started Household of Faith Ministries in 1979, and by 1989 the rapidly growing ministry moved into a converted supermarket and changed its name to Christian Life Center.

In addition to leading the Lord's work as senior pastor of Christian Life Center, he joined the board of Christian Men's Network in 1990. In the six years that followed, he saw this organization grow to seventy-four international offices, with work in 150 nations. In 1993 Rev. Bernard added the responsibility of opening the Brooklyn Preparatory School to his ministry duties. Then in 2002 he became president of Christian Men's Network. He speaks frequently at universities, colleges, and to *Fortune* 500 companies, and in 1996 he spoke to an audience of one million Christian men on the mall in Washington, D.C. Rev. Bernard continues to lead his congregation of more than eighteen thousand members at New York's Christian Cultural Center, which is one of the largest independent churches on the East Coast.

Many years ago, A. R. Bernard's mother was led by her grandmother to believe in Jesus Christ and to place her trust in Him. Because of this A. R. Bernard is here today. His mother's strong faith led him at an early age to believe in a loving God and to accept His Son Jesus Christ as Lord and Savior. In those dark hours of disappointment, rejection, sadness, and failure she lived through, A. R. Bernard's mother could never have imagined the plan God had in mind for her baby boy. Because of the decision she made to give birth to him, countless people have come to believe.

God often does His work through just one person at a time, working through that person to make a difference in a dangerous world. One person makes the decision to surrender his or her life to God saying, "Yes, Lord, I'll go. Use me in Your service." Through those individual people, God makes a powerful difference in the lives of countless others. He has done this through the mother of A. R. Bernard, and then through A. R. himself. He has done it through Franklin Graham, Greg Laurie, Skip Heitzig, and Sami Dagher. Each of these men knew God in only a peripheral way until they were finally brought to their knees in submission before Him.

But what about you? Are you ready to respond to God's call? Are you ready to allow Him to make a difference in the lives of others by bringing His help and His promise of eternal life through knowing His Son, Jesus Christ, to people living in a dangerous world?

Before you turn the page, ask yourself these questions:

- Are you leading others to accept Jesus Christ as Lord and Savior?
- Is your life an example that will lead others to believe in Almighty God?
- Will God say to you on that day, "Well done, good and faithful servant"?

PART 4

The Courage to Live

chapter 10

The Desire to Live

For whoever desires to save his life will lose it, but whoever loses his life for My sake and the gospel's will save it.

—JOHN 15:12 NKJV

IT IS DIFFICULT TO IMAGINE the mindset of a person who does not want to live. Even in places where life presents a new struggle for survival everyday—a struggle to find food to eat, to find water to drink and to have safety from others who threaten bodily harm—people fight to overcome adversity in order to live.

While working in Kosovo after the war in that country, I met a surgeon named Dr. Fehmi Vula, who related to me the most incredible story of his own struggle to live. Arrested and charged with war crimes for having given medical care to soldiers of the Kosovo Liberation Army, he was placed in prison and subjected to unspeakable punishment. Dr. Fehmi told his accusers that he had only done what was required of him as a physician, to give care to those injured in the war, no matter who they were. He repeatedly told his accusers that he only wanted to help those wounded in the fighting by giving them medical treatment.

To hear his story of suffering is to be shaken, horrified at how unjust life can be and then reminded how intense the battle to live can become. I had noticed the two pale scars that encircled his wrists, which were permanent reminders of five and a half months of imprisonment. One afternoon, after finishing work at the hospital, he told me his story—one I will never forget.

> It all happened during the early months of 1998. The fighting was horrific. There were many casualties. On May 25, 1998, I was at work in the operating room when the Serbian police came for me. They took me to the police station for questioning.
>
> For over two hours I was asked one question after another. Soon the tone of my interrogators became increasingly harsh, and I found myself being accused of supporting terrorist troops because I operated on wounded soldiers of the Kosovo Liberation Army.
>
> "You do not understand," I said. "I have simply been faithful to my calling as a physician, being true to the Hippocratic Oath to 'do that which is good for my patients, according to my ability and my judgment and never do harm to anyone.'"
>
> The accusations continued, and during the whole interrogation a revolver was held to my head. Nothing I could say would satisfy the hatred of my accusers. They placed me in a basement room filled with the shadows of other men who had been arrested. There was no light, food, or water in the room, and I felt terrible pangs of thirst. With every breath I was able to inhale only dank, stale air.

It was necessary for me to remain standing and when, on the fourth day of my arrest, I was finally taken from the dark basement cell, my arms and legs were swollen to twice their normal size.

At that time they led me back to the interrogator's office where a bright light was aimed directly at my face, and the pain in my eyes was almost impossible to tolerate. For eight more hours I was interrogated.

When I failed to confess any crime, they put iron bracelets around my wrists and ankles and anchored me to the cement with a chain. For the next twenty days I was kept alone in total darkness in a cell that was as hot as a furnace.

Along with six other prisoners, I was finally taken from my prison cell. We were bound hand and foot and loaded into a small, enclosed, metal luggage trailer. It was so cramped that none of us could move. During the middle of July the humidity was high, and the sun never stopped blazing. With no ventilation, the air in the metal trailer became thicker and hotter, causing the six of us to struggle for each breath.

Two of the other prisoners were young men, seventeen and nineteen years old. They had known me previously as a physician. Now they knew me as a fellow prisoner, a person with whom they would likely die. One of them asked, "When we die, will our brains stop first, or will our hearts stop beating? If our hearts stop beating first, surely we will still be aware when we have become dead."

The minutes wore on, and my head began to throb. I prayed that my answers to the questions of the other men were convincing as I told them, "Neither our hearts nor our brains are going to stop functioning. We are not going to die. We are going to survive, because they are taking us to a better jail. We are going to survive."

The two young men who were seated on each side of me lost consciousness and slumped against me. My own consciousness began to fade. When all hope seemed lost, I heard voices and shouts saying, "Let's go." The armored vehicle which pulled our trailer started to move, a small amount of fresh air entered through the door slit, and in that moment it seemed a gift more wonderful than I could ever have imagined. Hunched over inside that horrid trailer I called out, "No, I will not die. I will *live* for what is right!"

Dr. Fehmi paused briefly in telling me his story. Then he continued, relating the events of the next several months of his imprisonment. Eventually he was released pending rearrest to be taken to Belgrade to stand trial. He told me how, once released from prison, he returned to his work as a surgeon, doing all that he could to make a difference in the lives of others. But then on March 24, 1999, the Serb police had come to the home of his surgeon colleague and killed him in the presence of his family.

Then the following morning they came to kill me. As the police came through the hospital's main entrance, I rushed from my o ffice, leaving through a back door to the parking lot where a friend was waiting for me.

We went to my friend's house where a hole four-and-one-half-feet deep—just big enough for my body—had been dug for me. The soil was very damp, and I had only two fleecy lamb's skins, a piece of sponge, and a blanket to provide some warmth.

My friends covered the hole with wooden planks, followed by a sheet of nylon, and then a layer of soil. Two small shafts were left open to provide air for me to breathe. The two men then smoothed the soil to help avoid detection of my hiding place, and fled into the darkness.

After spending four days buried, I heard sounds of hands scraping against the boards overhead and my wife's voice.

"Our friends have fled. The Serbian Police were too near, so they left, but first they told me where you were hidden. I have come to free you. We must take our children and flee as well. There is very little time. The police killed some people near our house, and they will kill us if we don't flee."

My wife pulled and I pushed until we both felt the ground above me begin to move. Then suddenly my wife's outstretched hands gripped mine. A wall of earth broke free and standing above me, her arms bathed in mud and rock, was my beautiful wife, my sweetheart, the mother of our children, risking her life in order that I might live.

She told me there was a truck twenty meters away from the place where I had been buried. I walked as fast as I could with my stiff and painful legs, and with help my wife, my children, and I got into the truck. There were more than a hundred women and children in the escape truck, and as I lay down in the center of the truck bed, they covered me somehow with their bodies. We traveled over fifty curving miles to the Albanian border, and to freedom.

With the ending of the terrible hostilities in Kosovo, Dr. Fehmi Vula and his family have been able to return to their home, a home rebuilt after Serbian police bombed and burned it during the war. He is once again the chief surgeon at Gjakova Hospital, making a difference in the lives of his patients.

His compelling story is one of heroic struggle to live here and now, but in John 3 we read about Jesus telling a nonbeliever, Nicodemus, what is required of one who wishes to live for eternity. Jesus described the two ways to live: one is physical or "of the flesh," and the other is "of the spirit," which is life eternal with our heavenly Father. Every person must decide whether to live only in and for this world, or also to receive God's gift of leternal life.

A Modern-day Job

While most people vigorously resist anything that threatens their ability to live as long as possible in this limited life, few seek the life that is for eternity.

Reyna Ponce freely gives to others the one thing she has to give—her testimony as one seeking to live both in this world and eternally with God. It is her prayer that through hearing her story, many others will also want to live eternally.

Reyna is sero-positive for HIV and lives in San Pedro Sula, Honduras. Several years ago life could not have been better as she fell in love and married a wonderful young man. Their marriage was blessed with the birth of two beautiful baby daughters.

When her mother-in-law became ill, she was admitted to the hospital where Reyna, a nurse, personally helped care for her. Reyna's husband also found an opportunity to show his love for his mother by donating the blood she would need during her operation. After the surgery, Reyna noticed that her mother-in-law's wound was not healing properly and that she was not improving as quickly as expected. Blood studies revealed her to be HIV positive, and eventually she died of AIDS.

Realizing the improbability of her mother-in-law's having become HIV positive in any other way, Reyna began to wonder if it could have occurred from the transfusion of her husband's blood. She encouraged him to be tested, and she also had her blood tested. Sadly, both she and her husband were found to be HIV positive. As they discussed how either one of them might have become infected with the deadly virus, Reyna's husband acknowledged having been sexually active with other women before they were married.

In January 1994 Reyna's husband became ill with an abscess in one of his lungs. He was taken to the operating room to drain this abscess, but during the surgery something terrible happened. First, there was an electrical power failure in the hospital, and then the back-up electrical generator failed. As the surgeon struggled to control bleeding in the near-dark operating room, he severely lacerated a major artery causing Reyna's husband to bleed to death on the operating table.

As in the story of Job, the life of this once healthy, happy, young woman had now become one of terror and loss. She was now a widow at age thirty-four raising two small daughters, both of whom, thankfully, tested HIV negative. And fortunately, Reyna has remained alive and seemingly well over the past nine years since first finding that she is HIV positive. During these years she has been doing everything she can to provide love and stability for her young daughters while trying to shield them from the stigma and the discrimination that goes with her being HIV positive.

Reyna Ponce has the love of Jesus Christ in her heart, and she has forgiven her deceased husband, who unknowingly infected her and his mother. Her love is also seen in the way she works to support herself and her two young daughters, acting as both mother and father to them. And her love is seen in the way she gives so freely of herself to others through her courage in standing up and saying, "I am HIV positive." By doing so Reyna is able to lead others to believe in Jesus Christ and, through God's grace, to receive His gift of life throughout eternity.

Reyna Ponce wants to live. She wants to be there for her daughters as they go through their teenage years and face the problems and temptations they bring. Since she is HIV positive, she knows this life is uncertain for her, but she knows she will live throughout eternity in heaven because she believes in God and has accepted Jesus Christ as Lord and Savior.

In John 3:3, Jesus told Nicodemus that each person must make the decision to be born again of the spirit, if they desire to receive God's gift of eternal life. Nicodemus appears to have been a good man, but Jesus told him that being good was not enough, saying, "Most assuredly, I say to you, unless one is born again, he cannot see the kingdom of God." Then He clearly stated the only way we can come to God, and receive His gift of eternal life, is through Him: "I am the way, the truth, and the life. No one comes to the Father except through Me" (John 14:6).

As we seek those ways in which we can make a difference in the world for God's glory, may we first show the love of Jesus Christ. We are called to give to others in their time of need, but that is not enough. We must also be diligent in proclaiming His gospel, so people everywhere will know they can live eternally by being born again. If you are not living your life in the fullest way possible, pray to God that He will lead you to do so.

We are grateful for the knowledge that the one true God is a loving God and that He is in control. We give thanks in knowing we can speak to Him and that He will hear us and respond to our prayers. And we give thanks to Him for sending His Son into the world to show us the way to live our lives and for providing the way for us to receive His gift of life eternal.

Before you turn the page, ask yourself these questions:

- How am I bringing help to my neighbors?
- Am I living my life as one who has been born again?
- Am I leading others to God and His Son so they may live?

chapter 11

Finding the Way to Live

But as many as received Him, to them He gave the right to become children of God, to those who believe in His name: who were born, not of blood, nor of the will of the flesh, nor of the will of man, but of God.

—JOHN 1:12–13

AFTER DINNER on Easter Sunday evening, our children Michael, Elizabeth, and Robert and their spouses, Susie, Paul, Sheryl, and our five grandchildren, gathered around Sylvia and me and presented a beautiful photo album to us as an early forty-fourth wedding anniversary gift. Each had taken part in preparing the album, filling it with color photos taken from the time we were married, chronicling our many trips and good times as a family. Then our little granddaughters, Kaitlin, Amelia, Julianne, and Stephanie climbed up on our laps to give us kisses and to say, "I love you, Granddad and Grandy." Fourteen-month-old Alexander obviously wasn't into this "kissing stuff," but he toddled over to hug our legs and lay his head on our knees. Family times like these are wonderful and memorable and cause one to want to live forever.

Unfortunately, life isn't so wonderful for many families in the world today. Love may be the same, but the problems many people face in our dangerous world today present daily challenges.

For example, a woman I will call Mama Muzumundo is having to face some major difficulties during these senior years of her life.

Mama Muzumundo lives at the end of a long, bumpy, dusty road in a village in Africa, and her story is typical for perhaps hundreds of thousands of elderly people there. Her little two-bedroom house is old and in need of repair. Its walls and floor are crisscrossed with cracks. During the rainy season water drips and sometimes pours into her little home through its leaky tin roof.

Life has never been kind to Mama Muzumundo, but she has been content and happy with what she has had. She has always counted being surrounded by her family and by friends in her village as a special blessing. They, like Mama Muzumundo, have spent their lifetimes working the hard, red soil on their little farms to grow the food necessary to sustain them.

Mama Muzumundo certainly never looked forward to growing old, and she even dreamed that one day she would not have to work so hard and would be cared for by her grown children. That day will never come because a silent killer called AIDS came to the continent of Africa, bringing with it terrible sadness and suffering, separation among families, and ultimately death. Over a few short years she saw each of her eight grown children die of AIDS. She was left to care for, feed, and raise her grandchildren, ages two to fourteen. Her prayer is that she will live long enough to see each one of them reach adulthood and be able to care for themselves. For now her only source of income is from swinging a sledgehammer to break rocks into gravel for construction projects.

But there is more to the story of the responsibility Mama Muzumundo has assumed in her golden years. She has become "Mama" for children of several nieces and nephews who died from AIDS. And at age seventy, she has also invited other AIDS orphans to come into her little house and call it home. These were children she found wandering alone and destitute in the dusty streets of her village. In fact, she is now "Mama" to a total of twenty-two children.

Through God's blessing, her story of sadness has become a story of inspiration for countless other people. In spite of advancing years and the heavy responsibility she must now carry, God has blessed her with a sense of hope. With the children to care for, she has a new feeling of purpose and fulfillment. She has heard God's voice calling her to new responsibilities that are likely to continue for the rest of her life.

Mama Muzumundo is very poor in terms of things of this world, but she is rich in love and has a willingness to give to these children the blessing of a home and a means of survival. Through her wonderful example, she is leading them to believe in God and praying they will make the decision to live, by not becoming infected with HIV.

A Lesson in Grace

Half a world away there is a man who, like Mama Muzumundo, is in his seventies and has also been powerfully impacted by AIDS. His name is Dr. Harvey Elder, and he is a professor of infectious diseases at Loma Linda University Medical Center.

Harvey Elder grew up on a farm and was surrounded by the love of his Christian family. When he was twelve years old, he accepted Jesus Christ as Lord and Savior. In the years that followed, Harvey worked hard, studied hard, graduated from medical school, and became a specialist in infectious diseases, rising to the academic rank of professor.

Dr. Elder tells how he tried to live his life as he felt God would have him do, which sometimes caused him to be judgmental.

> I looked down on mere mortals who did not share or meet my standards. In 1981 I heard of an epidemic spreading among homosexuals and injection drug users, and in my thoughts I severely condemned those who practiced the risk factors for HIV. A few months later I saw my first patient with AIDS. Even though I tried to be nice to him, in my heart I didn't like him, and he returned the favor!
>
> Then a young man named Richard came under my care. He was suffering with AIDS, and as I cared for him we would often talk. He told me he had nine siblings, three sisters and six brothers, all injection drug users. Five of the seven boys were gay, one had already died of AIDS, another probably had the disease, and then there was Richard. Each child in his family had been physically, emotionally, and sexually abused by their father.
>
> As I sat across my desk from Richard, God caused my mind to begin to grapple with a terrible truth. *What had I done to deserve growing up in a loving family? Why had my entire life been so blessed, when this young man's life had seen one tragedy of abuse after another?* I began to realize I had been given a grace by God and that Richard had not received that grace. I also realized I could make it more fair by giving my grace away, allowing God to use me in helping Richard to live abundantly and for eternity.
>
> About three o'clock one morning I awakened with a very clear question before me: *Harvey, if Christ were an infec-*

tious disease physician working at Loma Linda University Medical Center, what would He do? The answer came to me very quickly: *He would care for people whom others had passed by, or wished to pass by, like those who suffer with AIDS!* My life changed as I prayed for God's leading that I might have the love, the compassion, and willingness to serve others the way Jesus demonstrated, and that through my efforts they might be able to live.

During a lifetime of studying God's Word, I had always despised reading about the Pharisees, especially the story of a well-known Pharisee named Simon, as told in Luke 7:36–48. Now from this story, I have a new vision for how I should serve patients suffering with AIDS. The Bible tells how Simon gave a feast, and Jesus was an invited guest. When Jesus arrived at Simon's house He was not extended the customary courtesies of that day. But a woman of ill repute, who heard Jesus was at Simon's house, came there to find him and treated Jesus with respect. She stood at His feet weeping, and she began to wash His feet with her tears, wiping them with the hair of her head, and then she kissed His feet and anointed them with fragrant oil (v. 38). Observing this, Simon "spoke to himself, saying, 'This man, if He were a prophet, would know who and what manner of woman this is who is touching Him, for she is a sinner'" (v. 39).

Knowing Simon's thoughts, Jesus said, "Simon, I have something to say to you . . . There was a certain creditor who had two debtors. One owed five hundred denarii, and the other fifty. And when they had nothing with which to repay, he freely forgave them both. Tell Me, therefore, which of them will love him more?"

Simon responded, "I suppose the one whom he forgave more."

And Jesus answered Simon, "You have rightly judged."

Then, while looking toward the woman, Jesus said to Simon, "Do you see this woman? I entered your house; you gave Me no water for My feet, but she has washed My feet with her tears and wiped them with the hair of her head. You gave Me no kiss, but this woman has not ceased to kiss My feet since the time I came in. You did not anoint My head with oil, but this woman has anointed My feet with fragrant oil. Therefore I say to you, her sins, which are many, are forgiven, for she loved much. But to whom little is forgiven, the same loves little."

Then Jesus said to the woman, "Your sins are forgiven."

In this story I can see the love for Jesus exhibited by a woman who had lived a particularly sinful life. She must have heard Jesus teach and saw in Him an opportunity for forgiveness and hope in her life. I can also see the power of the love of Jesus being shown in a very gentle way as He spoke to the Pharisee about the woman, and then in the loving way in which He forgave her sin and sent her on her way with new hope.

This story shows that we are to approach each person whose life we touch with the love of Jesus, not with the attitude of judgment shown by the Pharisee. The woman in the story came to Jesus because she believed Him to be a person of love who would accept her for who she was. By accepting nonbelievers who suffer with AIDS, we will have an opportunity to share the gospel and lead them to believe and live according to God's laws. Through sexual abstinence before marriage and faithfulness in marriage, there is little risk of becoming infected with AIDS.

Dr. Harvey Elder is making a difference by caring for patients who suffer with AIDS. Mama Muzumundo is making a difference by caring for children who have become the innocent victims of AIDS. And in California, a doctor works untiringly to save the lives of babies born to HIV-positive mothers.

One at a Time

Dr. Arthur Ammann is a committed Christian physician and professor of pediatric immunology at the University of California Hospital in San Francisco. He hadn't planned to become involved in AIDS. However, in 1982, while caring for sick children, he reported the first case of AIDS in a child. This was when little was understood concerning this new disease, and his young patient had become strangely ill after receiving a blood transfusion as treatment of her hemophilia.

Dr. Ammann has written of his journey since 1982,

> I look back with wonder at the direction in which God has led me over the forty years of my medical career. I cannot say it has been what I anticipated those many years ago when I applied for acceptance to medical school. He has taken me into areas that I would not have ever dreamed probable. Now as I travel to some of the poorest countries in the world and see firsthand the extraordinary needs of His creation, He has given me a better understanding of why so much of His Son's teachings were directed to the poor and the suffering.

My journey has not been without questions. I have had to struggle with the meaning of pain and suffering, and in particular the scourge of AIDS, a disease that disproportionately brings economic, social, and health discrimination against the women and children who suffer with it or because of it.

One of the most common modes of HIV transmission is from infected mother to newborn infant during childbirth. As a professor of Pediatric Immunology, my heart has always been with saving lives and improving health for babies and small children. Thus, during the early years of our struggle to combat AIDS my prayers were especially that we would find a way to save lives of infants born to HIV-infected mothers.

The drug AZT could reduce the number of infected infants by 60 percent, but this costly treatment was not feasible in developing countries where the AIDS epidemic has been causing eighteen hundred new infections in infants each day. In 1999, a new drug called Nevirapine was found to reduce the numbers of cases of HIV transmission between infected mother and newborn infant by 50 percent, and the cost for saving each of these babies lives was just eighty-five cents!

A real transition point occurred in my life when, during a trip to India, God spoke to me through my reading of His Word as recorded in Matthew 8:1–4. In these passages Jesus reaches out and heals a leper who had come to Him. There must have been thousands of lepers in Israel at that time, but He heals only one.

After reading this passage, I got up and looked out the hotel window and saw schoolchildren entering the playground of a school, happy and eager as they waded through the water and the mud from a flooding rain the previous evening. These were but a few of the tens of millions of children living in India, but I saw each one of them as important, just as Jesus sees them. Then I understood what God asks of us. Each one of us is to reach out and touch the life of *just one person at a time*, showing God's love. Then He calls us to give help and hope to them, sharing with them the gospel so that they might come to believe in Him and learn that through obeying God's laws they may live.

A short time after returning from India, I was invited to speak at a Presbyterian church in Berkeley, California, regarding how we as Christians can respond to the AIDS epidemic. In my message I told the congregation of that church about the massive numbers of babies being born each day to HIV-infected mothers. Then I told them how the lives of at least 50 percent of these babies could be saved with a single dose of Nevirapine for mother and newborn baby, for a total cost of eighty-five cents for each life saved.

The members of that one church responded to God's call by giving over $160,000 for the purchase of Nevirapine—enough to treat almost thirty-thousand HIV-infected mothers, preventing at least fifteen thousand of their babies from becoming infected and dying with AIDS.

It is exciting to see God at work through people like Mama Muzumundo, Harvey Elder, and Arthur Ammann, leading them to reach out with His love and a helping hand to just one person at a time. Through committed Christians like these faithful servants who have said, "Yes, Lord, I'll go to do your work; send me," the church of Jesus Christ is being mobilized, charged, and empowered like never before. And Mrs. Muzumundo, Dr. Elder, and Dr. Ammann are all serving the Lord without even leaving the places where they live. Through their work they are beginning to make a difference in our dangerous world.

As Christians, we are able to bring more than a cup of water, a piece of bread, a healing medicine, and a helping hand to those in need. Because of the gospel of Jesus Christ, we are able to bring hope for the near future and for eternity.

A Man with No Hope

In John 5: 1–15, we read of someone else who had no hope. It is the story of the man healed by Jesus at the pool of Bethesda.

This poor soul, this forgotten man, this man with no hope had been lying there, along with others in a great multitude of the sick, the blind, the lame, and the otherwise infirmed, for thirty-eight years. The Bible tells us that periodically an angel would appear at the pool of Bethesda and go down into the waters and to stir them up. When this occurred, the first person to step into the waters of the pool was healed. This man needed just one person who would notice him and reach out and help him get into the pool. But, in thirty-eight years of lying there in a helpless condition, not one single person ever cared enough to stop and give him assistance. He was indeed a man without hope.

One day, as Jesus entered Jerusalem by the Sheep Gate, near the pool of Bethesda, he walked up to the infirmed man, and asked, "Do you want to be made well?" Imagine what it must have been like for this man.

Many people suffer with AIDS, with other diseases, from

famine and from terrorism and war. Perhaps they feel despised because their bodies are diseased and ravaged by a deadly virus, and perhaps they even despise themselves. Maybe they feel shunned because no one wants to get close enough to touch them, let alone help them. No matter what the cause of their suffering, millions of people worldwide must feel forgotten and without hope like the man who lay at the pool of Bethesda.

When Jesus asked the question, the man responded, "Sir, I have no man to put me into the pool when the water is stirred up; but while I am coming, another steps down before me."

Jesus was a master at getting right to the point. He said to the man, "Rise, take up your bed and walk." The Bible says, "Immediately the man was made well, took up his bed, and walked.'" Only Jesus was able to heal people in the same way He healed the man who lay infirmed near the pool of Bethesda. But we can give the love and compassion Jesus showed to those who struggle with illness and who wish to live.

The Bible tells us that God wants us to live physically and abundantly in this life so that we can bring honor and glory to Him. And He wants us to receive His gift of life eternal through knowing His Son, Jesus Christ, as Lord and Savior. The key to how we can achieve this is in the words Jesus spoke when He saw the healed man in the temple later. "See, you have been made well. Sin no more, lest a worse thing come upon you." God's laws clearly define what is right and what is wrong in terms of human behavior.

God has called us to make a difference, through bringing help to others in order that they might live. Some of the people He calls to His service in helping others have money to give. Some respond to His call by using the talents He has given to them. Some, like Mama Muzumundo, have only love and the fruits of their labors to give, but their God-given love is powerful.

God has a plan for your life, and perhaps it will be today that He calls you to begin to do that special thing in His service that He has planned just for you. Maybe He is preparing you now for a unique work that He will call you to do months, years, or even decades from now. I was fifty years old when I heard God speaking to me through Franklin Graham and responded to God's call for service in His name. Although he is now president and CEO of the Billy Graham Evangelistic Association and a leading evangelist, even Franklin was past thirty before he preached the gospel for the first time.

Remember to be still and listen so that you may know when God makes that special call upon your life, asking you to lead someone to Him through His Son. It may well be on this very day.

Before you read the last chapter, ask yourself these questions:

- Do you love God and your neighbors enough to lead others to believe?
- Do you show God's love and forgiveness by giving love and forgiveness?
- Are you ready to say, "Yes, Lord; use me" in leading others to truly live?

chapter 12

Encouraging Others to Live

A little while longer and the world will see Me no more, but you will see Me. Because I live, you will live also.

—JOHN 14:19

KAREN STONE GREGORCHUK was raised in the Jewish faith. She believes in God, loves Him with all her heart, soul, and mind, and loves her neighbors as she loves herself. Twelve years ago she accepted Jesus Christ as Lord and Savior, giving her life to Him. Karen's faith in God and her unquestioning belief that Jesus Christ walks at her side in every moment of every day has meant everything to her, especially during difficult years like this one. Her heart was broken a few months ago when her beautiful three-year-old granddaughter was found to have cancer in one of her eyes. The diseased eye was surgically removed, and after completing a course of chemotherapy, little Carrie's hair is just now beginning to grow back.

As she was dealing with the crisis of her granddaughter's cancer, Karen's father, already suffering with Parkinson's disease and heart disease, fell and fractured his spine and one leg. In the same week her mother fell and suffered a fractured pelvis. A short time later her father died, one day before his eighty-third birthday. Then her mother also passed away, and several months later her brother-in-law passed away.

You may be saying to yourself, *Wow! Karen Stone Gregorchuk has really experienced a difficult year.* And that is true. But the real crisis in her life started nearly two years ago when she felt a lump in her left breast. Worried that it might be something serious, she went to her doctor, and a biopsy was performed.

> I returned to see my doctor several days after the biopsy and sat nervously waiting my turn to be seen. When he called my husband, Bob, and me into his office, we sat down and then heard him say, "Karen, I am sorry to have to tell you, but you have cancer in your left breast."
>
> I had this terrible feeling of staring into the face of death. In the days that followed, they did all sorts of x-rays, scans, and tests, and thankfully, there was no evidence of my cancer having spread to the rest of my body. I felt overwhelmed with the desire to live and now felt I had a new lease on life.
>
> The treatment plan began with radical removal of my left breast one week later. Most of the lymph nodes from my left axilla were found to be cancerous, and my doctors told me it would be necessary to begin aggressive chemotherapy treatment. I felt frightened beyond belief and turned to my loving husband and friends at church who joined with me in praying to God for His help. I prayed that God would heal me, and that He would give the team of doctors treating me great wisdom. But my special

> prayer was that He would help me keep a good attitude and maintain my faith and trust in Him.
>
> Through my illness I experienced a special closeness to God. I found that because of the cancer my priorities changed. As I opened my heart, God filled it with His love in a way I could never have imagined. My prayers were for many things, but most of all my prayers were words of thanksgiving for the wonderful blessing of feeling God's presence in my life, and for the great gift of His Son, Jesus Christ, who died for my sins.

Good out of Bad

The effects of the chemotherapy treatment caused Karen to lose her once-beautiful hair. With radical removal of her left breast she felt unbalanced. For many weeks her extensive surgical site failed to heal. The chemotherapy caused her to feel weak and sick, but her strong faith in the Lord never wavered, and she never stopped doing everything she could to bring hope and encouragement to others.

In her third month of chemotherapy treatment, Karen wrote an e-mail to her many friends in which she said,

> I feel great overall, and very grateful in knowing so many people care about me and pray for me. The cards, e-mails, and meals we have received have been a special blessing. The love Bob and I have for each other and for each one of you grows every day. A disease like cancer slows you down and forces you to stop and smell the roses, and I thank God this has happened in my life. Through my illness, I have learned to live my life to the fullest every day. I have

> learned to turn to God in prayer, to read His Word, to share my faith with others, and to let my family and friends know I love them. Death is certain for all of us. No one gets out alive, but we have a choice of how to live our lives, and God has called us to do it with love, hope, peace, and faith.

Karen has survived her cancer for nearly two years and has no evidence of recurrence of her disease. Her hair has grown in again, and she has had very successful reconstructive surgery to build a new breast. The bounce is back in her step, and she is at work again with her husband, running their travel business and planning for the future.

She says of the deep, dark valley through which she has walked in her battle against cancer,

> It is a strange thing, having a disease that haunts and labels you. You don't want to be part of it, yet you are and you can't escape it. Even if you are unlikely to ever have a recurrence, you still wonder if the disease will reappear in your body. In my case the doctors do expect a recurrence. Even feeling as accepting of my disease as I do, as peaceful with it as I feel, and as grateful for every moment of life as I am, there is always some anxiety lurking just below the surface. This anxiety causes me to wake up very early most mornings, just to see if there is a new pain or some new feeling or symptom, that might be a signal of more difficulty.
>
> The reality is, there is absolutely nothing I can do about the fact I have been treated for cancer other than face life one day at a time. But something I can do, and have done every day, is pray to our loving God, thanking

> Him for His gift of life, telling Him I will live my life every day in a way that will show His love to others and bring glory to His name. None of us can know what tomorrow will bring. Still, we can find great peace in knowing that God loves us and that He has prepared a place for us to live with Him for eternity, if we believe in Him, and have accepted His Son, Jesus Christ, as Lord and Savior.

As we seek to make a difference in our world, there is much we can learn from the way Karen Stone Gregorchuk has dealt with the worries, uncertainties, and fears that have come with her battle against cancer. In meeting her challenges, Karen has placed her trust firmly in the Lord. She has allowed adversity to strengthen her love for God, and through this she has felt His love for her in a powerful way. Instead of walking through a deep valley of despair, she has chosen to climb to the mountaintop, doing so with the love and support of her husband, family, and friends. Rather than withdrawing into personal solitude in her time of crisis, she has opened up to people in her church and community and literally across the country, encouraging them to add their prayers in fighting the battle she must win if she is going to live.

In her heart Karen Stone Gregorchuk knows two great truths. One is that she needs God's help in meeting the challenges that face her. The second is that God is in control of her life, has a plan for her, and also has given her a promise that through knowing His Son, Jesus Christ, she will live in His presence throughout eternity.

As you and I watch the evening news and read newspaper accounts of suicide bombings, wars, and crimes against humanity, of evil despots and oppressive regimes, may we follow Karen's example by turning to God. May our most important daily conversations be with Him. May we walk in the footsteps of Jesus Christ, bringing love to a world filled with hate and bringing good to a world overwhelmed by evil. Through God's Word may we provide hope to those who know only fear and despair.

Step Forward; Be Counted

When I was growing up, there was a lady who faithfully attended our church every Sunday. She stood with others in the congregation to sing hymns, but she never uttered a sound. After the worship service one Sunday someone asked this faithful, committed Christian lady why she always stood in silence, hymnbook in hand, yet never joined in the singing. She responded, "I don't have a good singing voice, so I just stand there and enjoy the music and let other people do the singing."

As Christians we can no longer "stand there and enjoy the music" made by others. God is calling us to step forward and be counted, to *make a difference* in the lives of others. We stand face to face with the forces of evil, and we must be more than observers. People are trying to convince us God does not exist. Some seek to remove the words "In God we trust" from our currency and campaign to remove God's name from the Pledge of Allegiance. Others are sponsoring legislation to have crosses removed from hilltops and laws passed to disallow children the right to pray in schools. As believers in Almighty God and in His Son, Jesus Christ, we cannot remain apathetic. Are we going to stand idly by as the forces of evil deny the very existence of a loving God and ignore the fact that His Son came into the world to bring peace and forgiveness of sins?

On Sunday morning, December 7, 1941, the Japanese bombed Pearl Harbor, and President Franklin Delano Roosevelt responded by bringing the United States into World War II. Hundreds of thousands of men and women ceased whatever they were doing, said good-bye to their families and loved ones and took their place in the ranks of those who would fight for freedom. Thousands upon thousands of women donned slacks, rolled up their sleeves, and went to work aiding the war effort, each finding and filling their unique position to win a terrible war against the forces of evil. Tom Brokaw wrote a bestselling book entitled *The Greatest Generation* about the courageous, hardworking, committed men and women who joined together to win the battle against evil that was World War II. God is calling us to respond in our time, as those called "the greatest generation" responded, to wage a battle against sin and evil. To bring love to a world filled with hate, and to give to others in His name. He is calling us to lead others to believe in Him and in His Son, Jesus Christ.

Most of us will never be required to put on a military uniform and go to a faraway place to fight in a war for what we believe. The battle we have been called to fight is against hunger and sickness, against diseases like AIDS, tuberculosis, and malaria. It is the battle to overcome hatred with love and the challenge to replace want with plenty and to do all we can do to remove the yoke of oppression from those who do not know freedom. The Great Commission calls for us to proclaim the gospel to people everywhere, leading others to believe so they may come to know the joy of Christian living and receive God's promise of eternal life.

In spite of the dangers, the threats, and the conflicts that are before us, we live in a time of great opportunity. International travel and all of the instruments of the electronic age that make instant communication with others anywhere in the world have revolutionized our ability to reach out to others with the help they need. Satellite television enables evangelists to proclaim the gospel in a way never before possible.

The Effect of Good Leaders

On April 29, 2003, I was invited to the White House along with Franklin Graham, others from Samaritan's Purse and the Billy Graham Evangelistic Association, and a number of Christian leaders. You could have heard a pin drop as we sat in the East Room of the White House waiting for the announcement, and then it came: "Ladies and gentlemen, the president of the United States!" Standing with high respect we watched as President George W. Bush briskly entered the room. With passion in his voice, and confidence in his manner, he addressed the issue of AIDS, the plague of our time, calling upon Congress to enact legislation that would appropriate fifteen billion dollars for the fight against this terrible disease. One month later we were privileged to be in the State Department auditorium as President Bush signed the AIDS Initiative Bill that Congress had enacted in the full amount of fifteen billion dollars.

Before signing the bill, President Bush told how the U.S. Leadership Against AIDS, Tuberculosis, and Malaria Act of 2003 includes his Emergency Plan for AIDS relief. He said, "This great nation is stepping forward to help. The fight against AIDS is difficult, but not hopeless."

As I listened to the impassioned words of President Bush describing the need to bring help to the suffering people in our world today, I thought of the prophet Daniel. He too had been privileged to be in the presence of great power. Throughout his long and productive life, Daniel never turned from love for his sovereign God. He never failed to remember that "Wisdom and might are [the Lord's]," and "He gives wisdom to the wise and knowledge to those who have understanding" (Daniel 2:20–21).

We can learn much from Daniel, who lived in a dangerous world more than twenty-five hundred years ago.

During his formative years Daniel was blessed, but when Jerusalem was seiged, he witnessed the destruction of the city he loved. He also suffered the indignity of being taken captive to Babylon. Daniel never returned to his beloved home in Judah, but spent the last seventy years of his life in Babylon. God's amazing plan for Daniel's life called for him to live and work in the royal court of Babylon under four great kings. This presented a tremendous challenge and placed him in great potential danger. Yet the book of Daniel never mentions his having complained about the task to which God had called him.

We face many things that are similar to those encountered by Daniel. One focus of world conflict is the same holy city of Jerusalem that was once home to Daniel. Daniel's place of captivity in Babylon in ancient Mesopotamia was in what is now the country of Iraq where Saddam Hussein's evil rule threatened world peace. Iraq is located adjacent to Saudi Arabia, the homeland of Osama bin Laden and the birthplace of the evil terrorist movement known as Al-Qaeda.

Answers for how we can make a difference in our world today are found in the example of Daniel as he dealt with the challenges of his time.

- Daniel *loved God with all his heart, soul, and strength,* and he loved his neighbor as himself.
- Daniel *demonstrated God's love for others* through the way he lived his life.
- Daniel *took time to be still and listen,* and he was able to hear God's voice.
- Daniel said to God, *"Yes, Lord,* I'll do what You are calling me to do."
- Daniel *used the gifts God gave him,* and he showed wisdom, courage, and diplomacy.

- Daniel *risked his life to be faithful to God* by praying and giving thanks to Him.
- Daniel *lived a life of humility before God*, never having feelings of personal pride.
- Daniel *gave God the praise and the glory*, living his life as a servant of the Lord.
- Daniel *placed his trust in the Lord* when he was thrown into the lion's den.

The struggle between Christianity and Islam which characterized the Middle Ages has resurfaced. This has been precipitated by the war in the Middle East and by the rise in Islamic fundamentalism in Iran, through the evil reign of Saddam Hussein, and had been brought to crisis proportions by the terrorist movement of Osama bin Laden and Al-Qaeda.

The Call for Workers

The Bible tells us the reason that our world has been and will continue to be a dangerous place in which to live: the sinful behavior of man. Both the Bible and books of history are replete with accounts of wars and acts of terror from the earliest times of man's existence on earth.

In the twentieth century, World War I was fought because of German imperialism. The terrible evil unleashed after that war by Lenin and Stalin bore the name of Communism. In the late 1930s and the first half of the 1940s, Hitler's Nazism led to the Holocaust for the Jewish people in Europe. In the Pacific the imperialist ambitions of the Japanese government brought the attack on Pearl Harbor, as well as the unspeakable atrocities of World War II in the Far East.

With the end of colonialism, tribal wars in Africa have slaughtered millions of people. The fall of Communism led to wars of ethnic cleansing in the former Yugoslav Republic, and tensions in those countries continue to this day. During the last twenty years terrorism has silently but progressively reared its evil head. Because of recent attacks here and in other countries, our world will never be the same again.

We know how the story of man's existence on earth is going to end. Changing Bible prophesy is not ours to do and, therefore, is not the issue before us. God's laws have been clearly given for us to make a difference in our world for His honor and glory.

The question is, what is God calling us, as followers of Jesus Christ, to do to make a difference in the lives of others? And the rest of the question is, through our service to others, how can we share the gospel so that others might choose to accept Jesus Christ as Lord and Savior? The answers to these all-important questions are clearly recorded in the Bible. The teachings of Jesus are our manual, road map, and instruction book. We must decide whether we are going to do what God has called us to do.

Jesus stated the greatest commandment, saying, "And you shall love the Lord your God with all your heart, with all your soul, with all your mind, and with all your strength" (Mark 12:30). If we seek to make a difference, we are to start by obeying that commandment. We have been called to *love*, to *give*, to *believe*, and to *live*. By focusing our hearts and lives on these four words, we can make a difference in the lives of others.

God is calling us to a difficult task, but through His Word in Joshua 1:9 we hear Him encouraging us, "Have I not commanded you? Be strong and of good courage; do not be afraid, nor be dismayed, for the LORD your God is with you wherever you go."

Like Karen Stone Gregorchuk, may we rise above being terrified and discouraged as we face things that frighten us and will not go away. May we know that God will always be with us as workers in His harvest. May we not put off until another time doing those things that will bring help to others. May we not allow ourselves to "gather dust" because of complacency when so many others in the world suffer and experience great need.

Karen has dealt with her illness in a special way and says, "I realize how blessed I am. I have my life with God at the helm. I am blessed beyond comprehension. God truly gives us what we need and even more. Life is always good. All things are opportunities for growth, and God never lets us down." A favorite scripture that has given Karen hope, faith, trust and courage for living her life in such a positive way is Psalm 91:4: "He shall cover you with His feathers, and under His wings you shall take refuge."

Someone sent Karen a short story several years ago that has meant a great deal to her. The story offers a vivid word picture of the way Jesus loves us, and how through His gospel He gives us the protection of His widespread wings, if we will stay within the bounds of the cover they provide. The story goes like this:

> After a forest fire in a national park, forest rangers began their trek up a mountain to assess the inferno's damage. One ranger found a bird literally petrified in ashes, perched statuesquely on the ground at the base of a tree. Somewhat sickened by the eerie sight, he knocked over the bird with a stick. When he gently struck it, three tiny chicks scurried from under their dead mother's wings. The loving mother bird, keenly aware of impending disaster, had carried her offspring to the base of the tree and had then gathered them under her wings, instinctively knowing that the toxic smoke would rise and remaining pure air would stay on the ground, under her widespread

> wings. She could have flown to safety, but she had refused to abandon her babies. When the blaze arrived and the heat scorched her small body, the mother had remained steadfast. Because she had been willing to die, those she protected under her wings were able to live.

The Bible tells us God created us, He loves us, and He will protect us if we will stay under the widespread wings represented by His laws. The Bible also tells us that God sent His Son into the world to show us how to triumph over evil and that He was willing to die on the cross for the forgiveness of our sins. But, unlike the illustration of the mother bird who died so that those she loved might live, Jesus now lives! He died on the cross at Calvary for the forgiveness of our sins, but He is risen. He has gone to prepare a place for us in His Father's house, and the Bible says that if we choose to come to the Father through His Son, Jesus Christ, we will receive God's greatest gift: living in His presence throughout eternity.

Millions of people don't know about the good news of Jesus Christ. Many live with sickness and suffering, hunger and fear. Countless others live under constant threat from the forces of evil in our world. These are people who feel they have no hope. You and I have been called to reach out to people everywhere with a helping hand, a cup of water, a loaf of bread, shelter over their heads, and care for their wounds. But more than that, we are to share with them the gospel of Jesus Christ. Through us, they will know the truth of God's presence, His love, and His promise.

Today—right now—pray for God's leading in your life as you respond to His call to reach out in service to others. Then take time to prayerfully seek those unique things that God has planned just for you. As you begin to respond to God's call to love the world in

His name, you will find that your life will make a difference. Then you will discover that, because of your faithfulness in serving our loving God, He will bless you abundantly and make a difference in your life.

Afterword

ONE OF THE MANY PRIVILEGES God gives to each of us is the ability to make a difference in the world we live in day by day. Parents have the opportunity to instill character in the lives of their children; teachers have the chance to motivate their students to apply what they learn to better their futures; and physicians have the awesome responsibility of challenging their patients to take seriously health issues that confront them throughout life. Dr. Mel Cheatham is a man of character, motivation, and a faithful servant of the Lord Jesus Christ, who has committed himself to not only serving, but also challenging others to reach out to the needy and truly make a difference around the world.

All of us want our lives to count for something. During our walk along life's road, we all can make a difference—it's a choice. In this book, as you have read, Dr. Cheatham captured some authentic illustrations of people who have done just that. Mel himself is an example. I have traveled with Mel throughout war-torn countries and disaster areas and have personally watched as he has used his skills as a successful neurosurgeon to make a difference.

There is much to be said about men and women who respond to others in need out of hearts of compassion. Whether a person comes from a humble background or privileged, all are given opportunities to put self behind and respond as the Good Samaritan did long ago.

Make a Difference chronicles many of the experiences Mel has had in his life outside of the operating room. Because of his obedience to Christ and his willingness to be used by Him, Mel has met with heads of state in Asia, lectured in Iraqi hospitals, and comforted countless numbers of people unknown. Through it all, he has made a significant difference.

I hope these pages have been a great inspiration to you. I trust that this book has challenged you to consider how you can make a difference in your world. God has gifted you, too, with special abilities. I challenge you to use those God-given abilities to make a difference in the lives of people around you. That act of love and compassion will, in turn, make a difference in your own heart and life—a difference that draws you ever closer to the God whose grace has saved you. Why not reach out today to someone whose heart needs to be refreshed with the love and joy of Jesus Christ? When you do, you'll know with certainty that you, too, can make a difference.

—Franklin Graham

President & CEO, Samaritan's Purse

President & CEO, Billy Graham Evangelistic Association

Notes

Chapter 3

1. José Carreras, *Singing from the Soul* (Montrose, CA: YCP Publications, 1991).

Chapter 7

1. © 1996 Doulos Publishing (Administered by THE COPYRIGHT COMPANY, Nashville, TN) All rights reserved. International Copyright secured. Used by permission.

Chapter 8

1. Greg Laurie, *Why Believe* (Carol Stream, Ill.: Tyndale House, 2002). Used by permission.